Life of Edward, The Black Prince

EDWARD THE BLACK PRINCE

Life of Edward, The Black Prince
A Biography of One of the Most Notable Military Commanders of the Hundred Years War

Louise Creighton

Life of Edward, The Black Prince
*A Biography of One of the Most Notable Military Commanders
of the Hundred Years War*
by Louise Creighton

First published under the title
Life of Edward the Black Prince

Leonaur is an imprint of Oakpast Ltd

Copyright in this form © 2013 Oakpast Ltd

ISBN: 978-1-78282-084-0 (hardcover)
ISBN: 978-1-78282-085-7 (softcover)

http://www.leonaur.com

Publisher's Notes

The views expressed in this book are not necessarily those of the publisher.

Contents

Early Years of the Black Prince	11
Beginning of the French War	18
Cressy	26
The Siege of Calais	39
Chivalry	44
The Black Death	54
Renewal of War with France	62
Poitiers	67
Triumphal Return to England	80
The Peace of Bretigny	86
Edward III.'s Jubilee	91
The Black Prince in Aquitaine	99
Spanish Campaign	107
Failure in Aquitaine	115
English Politics	124
The Good Parliament	134
Death of the Black Prince	139
The First Years of Richard II.	145

In war, was never lion rag'd more fierce,
In peace, was never gentle lamb more mild,
Than was that young and princely gentleman;
. . . when he frown'd it was against the French,
And not against his friends; his noble hand
Did win what he did spend, and spent not that
Which his triumphant father's hand had won:
His hands were guilty of no kindred's blood,
But bloody with the enemies of his kin.
                         Shakespeare, *Richard II*. Act ii. Scene 2.

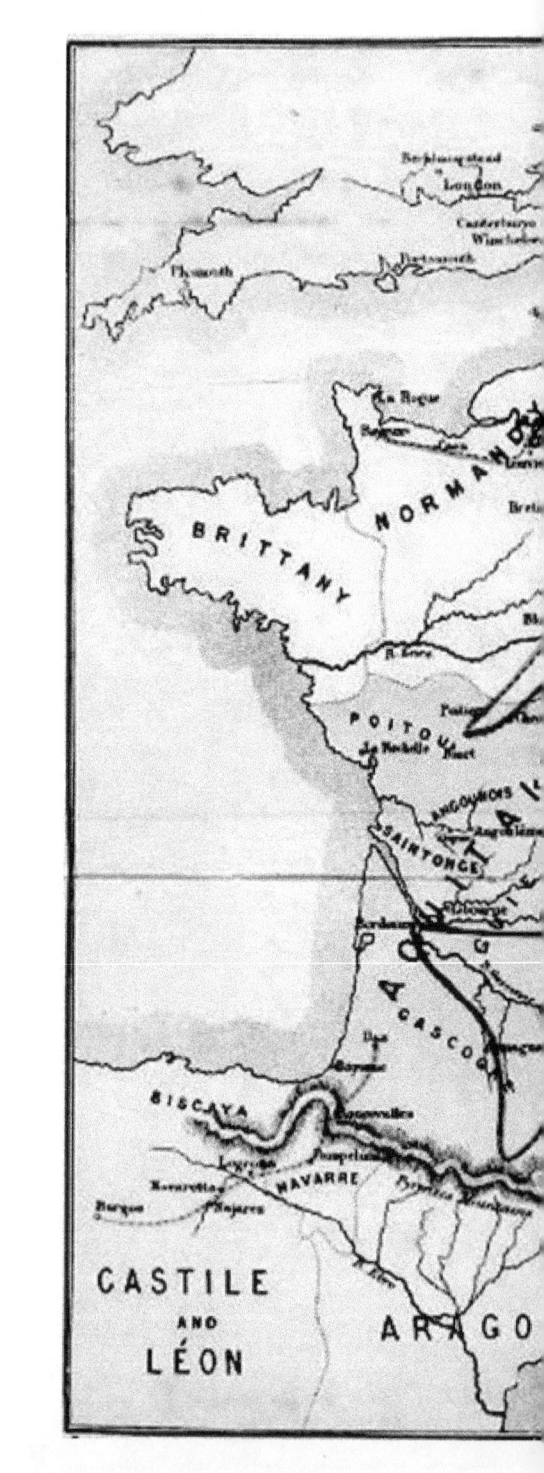

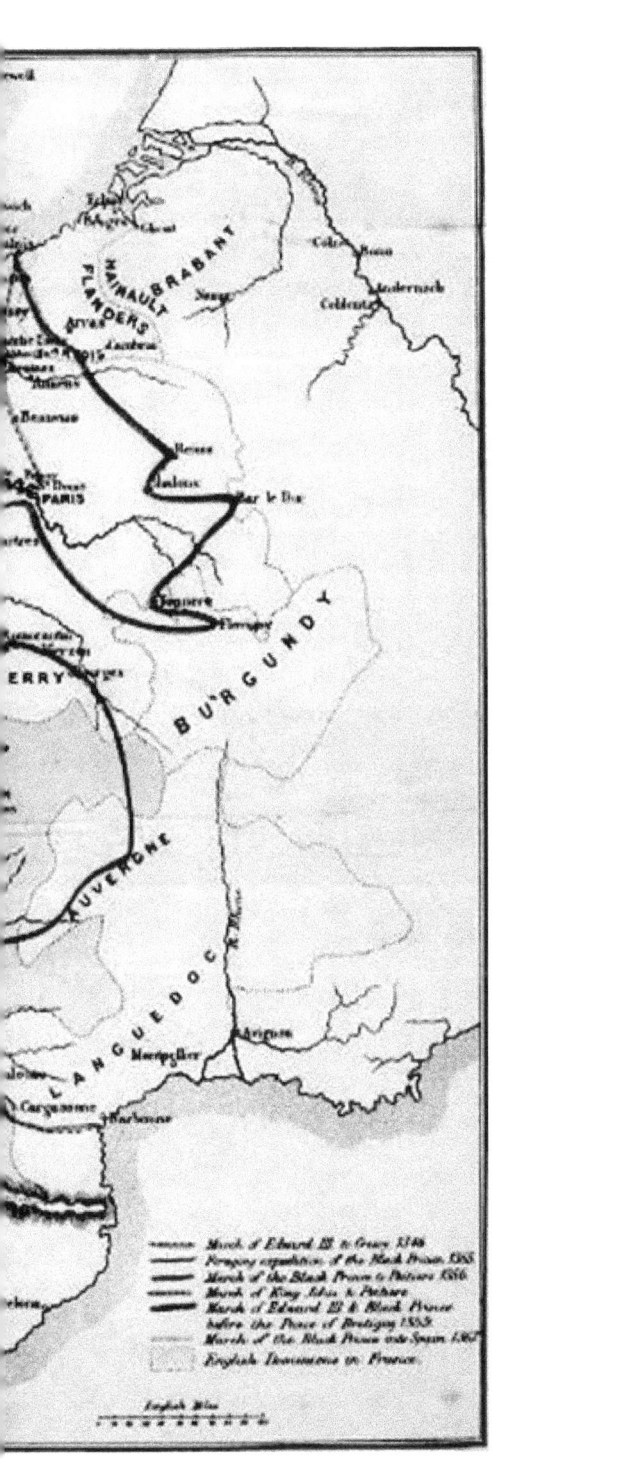

CHAPTER 1

Early Years of the Black Prince

On the 15th June, in the year 1330, there were great rejoicings in the Royal Palace of Woodstock. One Thomas Prior came hastening to the young King Edward III. to tell him that his queen had just given birth to a son. The king in his joy granted the bearer of this good news an annual pension of forty *marks*. We can well imagine how he hurried to see his child. When he found him in the arms of his nurse, Joan of Oxford, overjoyed at the sight, he gave the good woman a pension of ten pounds a year, and granted the same sum to Matilda Plumtree, the rocker of the prince's cradle.

Perhaps with Edward's thoughts of joy at the birth of his son were mingled some feelings of shame. It was three years since he had been crowned, and yet he was king only in name. He was nothing but a tool in the hands of his unscrupulous mother Isabella, and her ambitious favourite Mortimer. He was very young, not quite eighteen, and had not had sufficient knowledge or experience to know how to break the bonds within which he was held. But with the new dignity of father came to him a sense of his humiliating position. He would wish that his own son, on reviewing his youth, should have different thoughts of his father than he had.

He can hardly have borne to look back upon his own youth, with its shameful memories. He had seen his father, Edward II., by his dissipated life and his slavish devotion to his favourites, alienate the affection of his subjects, and provoke the barons to rise against him. Then, when peace had for awhile been restored, he had gone with his mother to France. He had seen her refuse to return to England at the king's demand; he had watched the growth of the disgraceful intimacy between her and Roger Mortimer, one of the rebel earls. At last, a powerless instrument in their hands, he had been taken by her and Mortimer to invade England, and Edward II.'s throne was attacked and overthrown by his own wife and son.

The rebellion was entirely successful. None were found to espouse the cause of the despised king. He was obliged formally to give up the crown to his son, and on the 20th January, 1327, Edward III., then only in his fourteenth year, was proclaimed king. All we know of the part taken by Edward III. himself in these proceedings is, that he refused to receive the crown without the sanction of his father. But he had no real power: all was in the hands of the queen and Mortimer. Before the end of the year, feeling insecure whilst Edward II. was still alive, they caused him to be secretly murdered in the castle where he was imprisoned. Soon after they married the young king to Philippa, daughter of the Count of Hainault, a union destined in every way to contribute to his happiness and to the good of the kingdom.

The power of Queen Isabella and Mortimer continued unchecked till the birth of Prince Edward. It was a troubled world in which the little prince first saw the light. For three years the English people had been subjected to a rule they detested, and their discontent had been gradually growing. One attempt at rebellion had been made by the king's uncle, Edmund Earl of Kent; but it had only ended in the execution of the simple, high-minded Earl. This had increased tenfold the hatred with which Mortimer was regarded. Edward III. felt that as a father he was no longer a mere boy, and could not continue to submit to his own degradation.

It was not difficult to find people ready and eager to enter into his plans. A conspiracy was formed, of which the queen and Mortimer seem to have had dim suspicions. They tried to avert the danger by keeping Edward with them in Nottingham Castle. But he succeeded in gaining over the governor of the castle, and a body of armed men was introduced at midnight through a subterranean passage. They broke into the room where Mortimer was, and after a short struggle made him prisoner. The queen, who was in the next room, burst in with agonized entreaties, "Fair son, fair son, oh spare the gentle Mortimer!"

Soon afterwards Mortimer was brought to trial, before a Parliament summoned by Edward, and was sentenced to be hanged. Queen Isabella was kept in honourable confinement till her death, twenty-seven years after.

Edward III. now took the entire management of affairs into his hands, and soon found that he had plenty to do. Whilst the little prince was still in his cradle, his father was already perplexed by the events which were to lead to those wars in which both played such a brilliant part.

Edward III.'s grandfather, Edward I., had cherished the dream of uniting under his own rule England, Scotland, and Wales. At times he had been very near the fulfilment of this dream; but Scottish love of independence had been too strong for him. The Scots found powerful leaders; they struggled fearlessly against apparently hopeless odds, and at last secured the throne to Robert Bruce.

The English however would not give up the hope of conquering Scotland. One of the most unpopular acts of Queen Isabella and Mortimer had been the conclusion of a peace with Scotland, called the Treaty of Northampton, in which they had recognised Robert Bruce as king. Edward III. therefore was acting quite in accordance with the wishes of his people when he interfered with Scottish affairs.

The moment seemed hopeful. Robert Bruce was dead, his son David was a mere child, and a new claimant to the throne had arisen in Edward Baliol, whose father in former days had struggled for the crown against the Bruces. Baliol was successful, and David Bruce had to fly to France. Then Edward demanded that Baliol should recognise him as *suzerain*, that is, should acknowledge the over-lordship of the English king, and do him homage as one of his vassals.

Baliol consented, and this in the end lost him his crown. The Scottish nobles, who had fought so bravely for their independence, would own no allegiance to a monarch who could tamely submit to the King of England; they revolted, and chased Baliol from the throne. It was then that Edward was called upon to interfere actively; he summoned an army, and marched against the revolted Scots; they were completely crushed at the Battle of Hallidon Hill, near Berwick. Berwick itself fell into Edward's hands, and remained part of the English dominions ever afterwards. Baliol was restored to the throne, and maintained there by Edward III.

The Scottish barons, however, still clung to the house of Bruce; they would not recognise Baliol, the sub-king of the King of England. They turned to France for help, and France was willing enough to listen to them and seize this opportunity of striking a blow at the growing power of the English Crown. Already, in the reign of Edward I., she had aided the Scots against the English; and it soon became clear to Edward III. that he could not hope for submission from Scotland until he had put an end to the intervention of France.

So we see that it is in the struggle between Scotland and England that we must look for the chief cause of the great French war, which was to drain the resources of both countries for a hundred years. We shall see, as we follow the course of events, how brilliantly this war opened, and how eager the English were to engage in it.

England, since Edward III. had become king in fact as well as in name, seemed inspired with a new life. The king was young and ambitious, anxious to promote his people's good, and eager to gain glory for himself. Commerce was extending on every side, and largely increasing the wealth of the country. National life beat vigorously, as we see, amongst other things, in the increased use of the English tongue. Formerly French had been the common language taught in the schools; but now it began gradually to fall into disuse, and before the end of Edward's reign the English language was to win its final triumph by the appearance of Chaucer, the first great English poet, and Wiclif, the first great English prose-writer. The English people were eager for some great undertaking, and from the very first the idea of the French war was extremely popular. The people wished it more than Edward himself, and the Parliament urged him to assert his claim to the French Crown.

It is not likely that anyone ever thought this claim to be serious, or considered it to be anything but a useful pretext for the war. Such as it was, Edward's claim to the French Crown came through his mother Isabella, granddaughter of Philip III. the Bold, King of France. Her three brothers had reigned one after another, and all died without male issue. On the death of the last, Charles IV., the crown passed to his cousin, Philip of Valois, son of Charles of Valois, the second son of Philip the Bold. Edward III., in asserting his claim, had to maintain, that though, according to the Salic law, females could not inherit the crown, they could transmit it to males.[1] He could never have seriously urged such a plea, if other causes had not led to a war with France, and

---

1. The following table illustrates Edward III.'s claim to the French Crown:

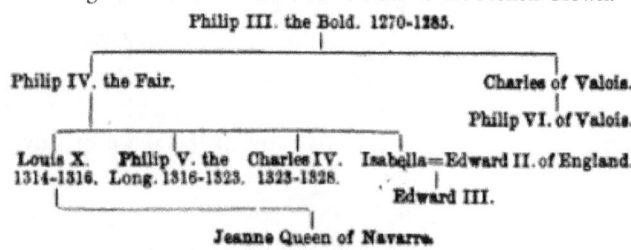

in time made it useful for him to assume the title of King of France.

There can be no doubt that Edward was grievously provoked by the French before he made up his mind to engage in war. The restless ambition of Philip of Valois produced a general feeling of insecurity. His pirate ships interfered with the trade of the channel. He made constant encroachments upon the English possessions in France, and frequently threatened an invasion of England, whilst he thwarted in every possible way Edward's policy with regard to Scotland. Under these circumstances it was natural for the English king to go to war, though if the war had not aimed at conquest it would have been better for England in the end. Edward III., however, was full of youthful ambition. He did not care to look into the future, but rushed into the war as if it had been a great tournament, in which he and his knights might distinguish themselves.

So active were the fears of French invasion during the first years of Edward III.'s reign, that we find orders for putting the Isle of Wight and the southern coast into a state of defence; and in 1335 the young prince was sent to Nottingham for safety. He must have been early accustomed to hear war talked of, and probably the chief part of his education was concerned with military exercises. We know little of his youth, except that he was educated under the direction of Dr. Walter Burley, of Merton College, Oxford, which, since its foundation by Walter de Merton, the Chancellor of Henry III., had produced most of the men distinguished in England for their learning.

Dr. Burley, on account of his fame for learning and piety, had been appointed queen's almoner; as his reputation increased at court, he was finally appointed tutor to the prince. In accordance with the custom of the times, many other young gentlemen were educated in common with Prince Edward, so that companionship might lend an increased interest to his studies. Amongst others, Simon Burley, a young kinsman of Dr. Burley's, was admitted to share these advantages. He became a great favourite with the prince, and in time was made Knight of the Garter, and was entrusted with the education of the prince's son, Richard of Bordeaux.

We can form a pretty good idea of the kind of education received by Prince Edward and his companions. Chivalry was then at its height, and it was necessary for every gentleman to be skilled in all knightly exercises. An accomplished knight must be endowed with beauty, with strength and agility of body; he must be skilled in music, be able to dance gracefully and run swiftly, to wrestle and sit well on horseback;

above all, he must be skilful in the management of arms, and must thoroughly understand hunting and hawking. In these accomplishments were young Edward and his companions trained, and we cannot doubt that he, who was the very type of the chivalric spirit in its highest development, early learnt to excel in all knightly exercises.

There exists a rhyming chronicle in French of the life of Edward the Black Prince, by the herald of Sir John Chandos, who was so constantly with the prince, that we may believe that his herald writes from personal knowledge of the prince's character. He says:

> *This frank Prince of whom I tell you,*
> *Thought not but of loyalty,*
> *Of free courage and gentleness;*
> *And endowed was he with such prowess*
> *That he wished all the days of his life*
> *To give up all his study*
> *To the holding of justice and integrity.*
> *And in that was he nurtured*
> *From the time of his infancy.*
> *Of his own noble and free will*
> *He learned liberality;*
> *For goodness and nobleness*
> *Were in his heart perfectly,*
> *From the first commencement*
> *Of his life and youth;*
> *And he was, it is well known,*
> *So preux (chivalrous), so hardy, and so valiant,*
> *So courteous and so wise,*
> *He loved so well holy church,*
> *With all his heart, in every form,*
> *The most holy Trinity,*
> *The festival and holiday.*

There is a tradition that Prince Edward studied at Queen's College, Oxford, and this may perhaps have been the case, as Queen's College was founded by his mother, Queen Philippa; but the story rests on no authentic evidence.

During his early youth various honours and dignities were bestowed upon him. He was made Duke of Cornwall at the Parliament held at Westminster in 1337. This is the first time that the title duke appears in English history. In 1338, when Edward III. was about to leave England to begin his war with France, he appointed his son Prince Edward to be guardian of the kingdom during his absence. As the prince was then but eight years old, this was naturally only a nominal office. It was not till 1343 that he was created by Parliament Prince of Wales.

CHAPTER 2

Beginning of the French War

The years from 1336 to 1338 had been spent by Edward III. in preparations for war. He had been endeavouring to gain allies amongst the princes on the continent, his idea being to unite against France the rulers of the small principalities that lay to its north, such as Brabant, Gueldres, Hainault, and Namur. He also succeeded in gaining the alliance of the Emperor Louis of Bavaria. But his most important ally was Jacques van Arteveldt, the man who then ruled Flanders with the title of Ruwaert.

The condition of Flanders at that time was very strange. Since 877 Flanders had been ruled by a long succession of counts, who had done homage to the kings of France for their country. The peculiar circumstances of the country, its mighty rivers, whose wide mouths afforded safe harbours for the ships, combined with the industry of the people, had early made Flanders important as a commercial and trading country. During the absence of the counts on the crusades, the towns had won for themselves many important privileges, and were really free communes, owning little more than a nominal allegiance to their duke. The kings of France eyed this wealthy and thriving province with great jealousy, and eagerly watched for an opportunity of asserting their authority over it.

But till 1322 the people and their counts had been firmly united in resistance to France. Only with the accession of Count Louis de Nevers did the aspect of affairs change. This count had been brought up in France, and was imbued with French interests. He objected to the power and independence of the Flemish towns, and sought to oppress them in every way. He governed by French ministers, and called in French help against his own subjects. Then, when the people were oppressed, their industries ruined, their commerce at a standstill by the tyranny of their count, they found a leader in Jacques van Arteveldt, who showed them the way to liberty and prosperity. Against the firm union formed by the towns the Count of Flanders was powerless, and fled to the Court of France.

Under Arteveldt's care commerce and manufactures flourished, peace and prosperity reigned in the land, whilst there was no question of actual revolt from the authority of the count. Arteveldt only wished to show that the liberties of the people must be respected. Flanders was the great commercial centre of the Middle Ages, where merchants from far distant countries met and exchanged their goods. Arteveldt conceived the great idea, in which he was far beyond the intelligence of his time, of establishing free trade and neutrality as far as commerce was concerned. He was an important ally for Edward III. for many reasons. It was necessary for the interests of both peoples that Flanders and England should be friends; for in Flanders England found a sale for her wool, then the great source of her national wealth.

From England alone could Flanders obtain this precious wool, which she manufactured into the famous Flemish cloth, and sent to all parts of the world. Edward III. recognised the wisdom and greatness of Arteveldt, and concluded a strong alliance with him for the benefit of both parties. On all occasions the English king treated the simple *burgher* of Ghent as an equal and a friend. It is not impossible that he gained in his intercourse with Arteveldt that feeling of the importance of commerce and industry which exercised so great an influence upon his legislation, and gained for him the title of the Father of English Commerce.

It was on the 16th July, 1338, that Edward III. sailed for Flanders. His first object was to meet his allies, the various princes of the Netherlands. He did not find them very eager for active co-operation in his undertaking. He determined to visit the emperor in person, so as to prevail upon him to take an active part in the war. With this view he travelled up the Rhine, stopping first at Cöln, then a thriving commercial city, enjoying active intercourse with England. Here Edward stayed some days in the house of a wealthy burgher; the time passed in merriment and festivities, the king receiving visits from all the chief citizens. He visited most of the churches, and made offerings at the various altars; to the building fund of the great Cathedral he gave £67, a sum equal to £1,000 of our money.

From Cöln he proceeded up the Rhine, his whole way being marked by continual festivities. At Bonn he stopped with one of the canons of the cathedral, at Andemach with the Franciscans, and finally, on the 31st August, he reached Coblentz, where the German Diet was assembled. The emperor received him in state in the market-place, seated on a throne twelve feet high, and by his side, though a little lower, was a seat for Edward. Around them stood a brilliant assembly; four of the electors were there, and wore the insignia of their rank. One of the nobles, as representative of the Duke of Brabant, held a naked sword high over the emperor's head; 17,000 knights and gentlemen are said to have been present.

In the presence of this imposing gathering Edward III. was created Vicar of the Empire for the west bank of the Rhine. In spite of this journey he obtained nothing from the emperor but this empty title. On his return to Flanders he was so short of money that he had to pawn the crown jewels to the *Bardi*, the great Florentine merchants at Bruges. The allies were slow in bringing their forces into the field. Van Arteveldt refused to give Edward any active help, because of the oaths of fealty by which the Flemings were bound to Philip of Valois. At last Edward succeeded in collecting an army of 15,000 men, and met the French before Cambrai. The two armies parted without a battle, and Edward returned to Hainault. This fruitless campaign had exhausted his resources without gaining any result. He grew more anxious than ever for the help of Flanders, and made new proposals to the towns with magnificent offers. Arteveldt at last consented to help him, if he would assume the title of King of France; then the fealty which the towns owed to their suzerain could be transferred from Philip of Valois to Edward.

This, then, was the real cause of Edward's assuming the arms and title of the King of France; he did it only that he might gain the active help of the Flemings. As their suzerain he confirmed all the privileges of the towns, and granted them three great charters of liberties. These charters bear the impress of Arteveldt's mind, and are an expression of his commercial views. They proclaim liberty of commerce, the abolition of tailage (that is, of taxes upon merchandise), and a common currency. They guarantee also the security of merchandise, as well as of the persons of the merchants. The wool staple was fixed at Bruges; that is, Bruges was to be the place where alone wool might be imported, and be sold to the Flemish merchants. Edward returned to England to obtain the confirmation of these treaties by Parliament, as Arteveldt would not be content unless the Commons of England gave their consent to them.

During his absence Queen Philippa remained at Ghent, and there gave birth to her third son John, who, from the city of his birth, was ever afterwards called John of Gaunt. Queen Philippa also acted as godmother to Arteveldt's son, who was called Philip after her, and afterwards became famous, like his father, for defending the liberties of his country, though he did not show his father's wisdom and moderation.

Edward III. obtained from the Parliament at Westminster the confirmation of his treaty with the Flemish towns, and also a new grant of supplies. This grant was for the most part in kind. The king was to have the ninth lamb, the ninth fleece, and the ninth sheaf; that is, in reality, a tenth part of the chief produce of the kingdom; for the tithe had first to be paid to the church, and so the ninth part of the remainder equalled the tithe. He was also allowed to levy a tax on the exportation of wool for two years. It shows the great popularity of the war that so large a grant was agreed upon. We also see the increasing power of Parliament, from the fact that Edward III. did not venture to impose any tax without its consent.

But in spite of all these grants Edward was still considerably in debt. He owed £9,000 to the merchants of Bruges and £18,100 to the association of German merchants in London, called the Hanseatic Steelyard, which had existed certainly since the time of Henry III., and had always been specially favoured by the English monarchs. But the merchants were always willing to lend him money, in return for the facilities which he gave to commerce. He was still obliged to pawn the crown jewels—his own crown was pawned to the city of Trier, and Queen Philippa's to Cöln. Orders had to be given for the alteration of the royal seal; the lilies of France had to be incorporated with the leopard of England.

Meanwhile the French had gathered a large fleet, composed principally of Genoese ships, and were threatening the Flemish coast. There was danger of their cutting off intercourse between Antwerp and England. It was necessary for Edward to set off without delay. He hastily collected a fleet of some 200 sail, and started from Orewell, a port in Suffolk, on 22nd June, 1340. When the English fleet neared Sluys they saw standing before them, as Froissart tells us, "so many masts that they looked like a wood." This was the French fleet waiting to dispute the passage of the English. When Edward heard who they were, he exclaimed:

I have for a long time wished to meet with them; and now, please God and St. George, we will fight with them; for in truth they have done me so much mischief that I will be revenged on them if possible."

The English fleet was arranged in order of battle. The strongest ships were put in the middle; between every two ships manned with archers was a ship of armed knights; the wings were mostly composed of archers. Great care was taken for the safety of a large number of noble ladies who were going to attend the queen at Ghent, picked men being chosen to guard them.

The French force was greatly superior to the English, as they possessed nineteen ships of very large size, most of which had been captured from the English the year before, when the French had attacked the English ports. The French formed themselves into four long lines; their ships were firmly fastened together with chains and ropes. The French admiral, considering his position impregnable, determined to remain on the defensive, and refused to listen to the advice of the Genoese commander Barbavara, and advance to the attack. The French were soon enveloped in a shower of English arrows; grappling irons fastened the English ships to the French, and the fight became fierce. The great English ship, the *Christofer*, was recaptured from the French, and the English flag again hoisted upon her.

The French were hemmed in on all sides. In their rear they were threatened by the inhabitants of the coast, so that escape seemed impossible. Only at nightfall did the Genoese and some few French ships succeed in getting away in the darkness. The loss of the French was enormous, whilst the English suffered comparatively little, and captured a vast amount of booty and a large number of prisoners.

Great were the rejoicings for this victory. The news of it passed rapidly from mouth to mouth. The French pirates were destroyed, and once more the merchant could carry his goods across the seas without danger. In all the English churches thanksgivings were offered for the victory by royal command. Edward III. had himself been slightly wounded in the battle, but still his first act on landing was to go with his knights on a pilgrimage to Our Lady of Ardembourg to give thanks. He then proceeded to Ghent, where he found his queen with her new-born baby.

Edward III. hoped to be able to follow up this naval victory by striking a decisive blow on land. The deputies of the Flemish towns and his other allies met him at Ghent, and the Flemings agreed to aid him, if he would help them to get back Artois, which had formerly belonged to Flanders, but had been treacherously taken from them by Philip IV., King of France. In five days the towns had levied 140,000 foot soldiers, who all agreed to fight without pay in this war. Thus reinforced, Edward marched to Tournai, which he completely invested. Philip advanced from Arras to relieve the town.

Discontent had already broken out in the confederate army. The Flemings were not professional soldiers, but were the burgers and handicraftsmen of the towns who had turned out to defend their own hearths and homes, marching under the banners of their different gilds. They were soon eager to get back to their shops and their looms. Philip's sister, Jeanne of Valois, a nun at Fontenelle hard by, appeared between the two armies as peacemaker, and a truce was agreed upon. Jacques van Arteveldt succeeded in obtaining most advantageous terms for the Flemings. With the habitual selfishness of a commercial and industrial people, having brought matters to a satisfactory conclusion for themselves, they thought no more of Edward's interests. He, too, had to agree to a truce for nine months, and to retire a second time without striking a decisive blow. He had expended vast sums of money in these two campaigns, and had gained nothing. He had only learnt one lesson, and that a very important one—that it was no use depending upon allies, and that henceforth he must trust to himself alone.

The truce between France and England had been concluded at first for only nine months, till 25th September, 1341, but it was afterwards prolonged till 1342. Edward soon found a new opening for attacking France, in the contest that was going on about the succession of the Duchy of Brittany. Edward III. determined to give his aid to De Montfort, whilst the other claimant, Charles of Blois, was supported by his uncle Philip. Here also, after awhile, a truce was agreed upon, which was to last till Michaelmas, 1346. A truce had also been made with Scotland, and David Bruce had returned to his kingdom.

Thus there was an interval of comparative peace; but each side was only waiting for an auspicious moment to begin the war again, and the French did not cease their aggressions upon Guienne. In spite of the large sums it cost, the English people were by no means weary of the war. The Parliament that sat in 1344 began by giving its opinion in favour of peace, if fair terms could be procured; but proceeded to grant the king supplies to enable him to continue the war. They begged him to finish it in a short time, either by battle or treaty. The nobles agreed to cross the sea and fight with him, and the clergy granted him the tenth of their benefices for three years. The king's cousin, the Earl of Derby, a brave and accomplished knight, was sent with an army into Guienne to recover the country which had been won by the French.

We must try to understand clearly what were at this time the possessions of the English in France. Under Henry II., the territory which the English king ruled over in France was greater in extent than England itself. Part of this, such as Normandy, belonged to the English kings, by virtue of their descent from William the Conqueror. Anjou and Tourraine had come to Henry II. through his father, Geoffrey of Anjou; the great Duchy of Aquitaine, consisting of seven provinces, he obtained as the marriage portion of his wife, Eleanor of Guienne. Thus he ruled over the western part of France, from the Channel to the Pyrenees, and held the mouths of the great rivers Seine, Loire, and Garonne. These vast dominions really made the Angevin kings, so called from their descent from Geoffrey of Anjou, foreign rather than English rulers. It was not therefore altogether to the disadvantage of England when Normandy and the other possessions in Northern France were taken from the feeble John by the King of France. The Duchy of Aquitaine still remained in the possession of the English. Once it was wrested from them in 1294 by Philip IV., King of France, but he soon had to restore it.

It is easy to imagine how anxious the French kings must have been to gain possession of this great duchy. A succession of able, unscrupulous kings, had been trying by every means to extend and consolidate their dominions. The kings of France had not at first been as powerful as many of their great barons, who ruled as hereditary and independent princes in their separate provinces, paying the king only a nominal homage. To reduce these barons to submission was the task laid upon the French kings for many generations. Little by little they got hold of the lands of their vassals and neighbours. Rivalry between France and England began from the first moment that the Dukes of Normandy became kings of England. It was increased when the Duchy of Aquitaine was added to the English dominions. Philip Augustus had won Normandy from John; it remained for his successors to win Aquitaine.

The Duchy of Aquitaine included Poitou, Limousin, Guienne, and Gascony. It extended towards the north almost as far as the mouth of the Loire, and towards the south to the foot of the Pyrenees. It embraced the fertile bed of the Garonne, at the mouth of which lay the great city of Bordeaux, whence the wine grown in the duchy was imported into England. Bayonne was another important port lying to the south of Bordeaux. It was here that the Earl of Derby landed when he was sent by Edward III. to recover the places which Philip had succeeded in winning in Guienne. His campaign was marked with brilliant success, and he soon won back all that had been lost.

Edward III. meanwhile determined to make another journey to Flanders, to strengthen his alliance with the Flemings. This time he took with him his son Prince Edward, who had now completed his education, and was to begin, at what seems to us the early age of fifteen, to take part in the active business of life. Van Arteveldt met his royal guests at Escluse, and the deputies of the towns also came to discuss the state of affairs. Froissart tells us that there was a proposal made by Arteveldt to set aside Louis Count of Flanders and make the Prince of Wales count in his stead. But this statement is not supported by other evidence, and does not seem to be in accordance with the views of Arteveldt, who never showed any desire to put aside the rightful count. Having assured himself of the friendship of Flanders, Edward returned to England with his son.

Only a few days after his departure his faithful friend Van Arteveldt was murdered at Ghent, in a disturbance caused by a furious faction of the populace. This murder was the act of a small party, not of the country. The government and administration of affairs remained as before throughout Flanders. The towns sent deputies to England to express to Edward III. their freedom from complicity in this murder, and their desire to maintain the English Alliance. The close commercial relations between the two countries, which had been established by the wisdom of Van Arteveldt, went on as before, and the English wool was still carried to the staple at Bruges to be sold.

CHAPTER 3

Cressy

During the years between the campaign in Flanders, which was ended by a truce on September 25th, 1340, and the campaign of Cressy, in 1346, Edward had been principally occupied in preparations for renewing the war. Peace negotiations had been carried on before Pope Clement VI. by commissioners appointed by the two kings; but as neither party wished for peace, it could not be expected that these would lead to any result.

The Parliament that sat at Westminster in 1343 had, as we have seen, relieved Edward III. from his pressing want of money by granting him new supplies, and he had been able to redeem his great crown from pawn. But he had borrowed so largely from the great Florentine merchants, the *bardi*, that his failure to pay his debt of 900,000 golden florins at the right time brought about their bankruptcy; and as they were the largest bankers in Florence, the whole city suffered greatly through their failure.

Once supplied with money, Edward had to turn his attention to raising levies for the war. The royal armies had long ceased to consist merely of the feudal militia, as this could not be used for any long campaign. According to feudal customs, the levies were only obliged to serve for forty days. Hence, though they could be used for a sudden attack upon a neighbouring prince, they were of little use to a king who wished to carry an army across the seas to invade a foreign country. The custom of commutation therefore had grown up; that is, of receiving money payments instead of personal service. With this money the king could then hire soldiers to fight for him as long as he chose to keep them. These hired soldiers were raised in the following way: the government appointed a contractor for every district, who agreed to furnish from that district a given number of men for a fixed pay. Sometimes the men enlisted voluntarily; but so many complaints were made by the Commons during Edward's reign of forced levies, that it seems as if compulsion was often used to obtain enlistments.

To raise soldiers for the campaign on which he was about to engage, Edward III. ordered the sheriffs throughout the country to summon every man-at-arms in the kingdom to attend personally, or else send a substitute. All landholders were to furnish men-at-arms, hobblers, and archers, in proportion to their incomes. All these men were paid for their service, and the rate of pay was much higher then than it is now. From this it appears that probably even the private soldier was taken from the smaller gentry or the rich yeomanry. This helps to account for the efficiency of Edward's army. It was through the valour of the common soldiers rather than through the prowess of his knights that Edward won his victories. On this occasion pardon was promised to criminals on condition of their serving in the war. Edward Prince of Wales was to collect 4,000 men from Wales, half lancers and half bow-men. All these levies were to meet at Portsmouth on October 9th, ready to embark. Let us try and get some idea of the nature of the troops collected at Portsmouth to form the army which was to invade France.

First in rank and importance were the men-at-arms. These were the knights with their esquires and followers. The esquires were the attendants upon the knights, and were generally young men of rank, serving their time till they should be raised to knighthood. The knights with their esquires and followers were all equipped alike in plate armour, and formed the heavy cavalry. Their chargers also were protected by plates of steel, and their armour was made so impervious that no weapon then known could pierce it. But its weight was so great that only to carry it exhausted the strength of the knights and crippled their power. Their arms were the lance, the sword, the battle-axe, or the mace, and they bore a shield for defence. Each knight who brought his esquires and followers into the field might bear his pennon, which was a long narrow ensign.

Some knights who were rich enough to have other knights in their service carried square banners. We can imagine the brilliant effect of a company of these knights in their burnished steel armour, often beautifully chased and inlaid with other metals, with their gay banners streaming in the wind. Many of them might be seen bearing a falcon on their wrist, so that amidst the fatigues of war they might occasionally refresh themselves with the chase. To them was reserved the place of honour in the battle; theirs are the deeds of prowess which the chroniclers delight to record. War was to them only a vast tournament, in which they might display their valour and strive to surpass their adversaries.

Next came the hobblers, the light cavalry, who were recruited from a rank inferior to that of the knights. Their horses also were inferior, and they were not so heavily armed.

But the real strength of the army lay in the third body of men, the archers, who of course fought on foot. It was to their skill and courage that Edward was to owe his victories. Shooting with the long-bow was a thoroughly English recreation. On holidays it had long been the custom for the yeomen to meet together to practise their skill by shooting at a mark. The kings did their utmost to encourage this pastime. In the thirteenth century every person possessing a revenue of above one hundred pence in land was obliged to have a bow and arrows in his possession. Edward III. feared at one time that the skill of the English archers was declining. He sent a letter to the sheriffs of London, in which he said, that:

> The skill in shooting arrows was almost totally laid aside for the pursuit of various useless and unlawful games, such as quoits, cock-fighting, football, &c.

He commanded the sheriffs, therefore, to see that the leisure time on holidays was spent in recreations with bows and arrows; so highly did Edward value the archer's skill. Of course, as there was no standing army, there could be no body of regularly-trained archers. The archers, like the other soldiers, were recruited from the people; and if the mass of the people were not practised in archery, there could be no hope of obtaining skilful archers. The bows used by them were six feet long, their arrows three feet. In shooting they drew their arrows to the ear, and could send them with good aim a distance of 240 yards. They carried their bows in canvas cases, so that they might not be wetted by the rain, or cracked by the sun. Edward III. had a body-guard of archers, 120 in number, chosen from the stoutest and most skilful men in the country.

The fourth body of men consisted of the remaining foot soldiers, who were mostly armed with lances. Besides these a large number of labourers of various kinds had to be engaged to follow the army. These men were pressed by the sheriffs, and in most cases were obliged to go against their will; for it could hardly be to their profit to leave their homes and their business to meet all the dangers of a distant expedition. There were the blacksmiths to repair the armour and shoe the horses; the masons to build the bridges; the rope-makers, carpenters, wood-cutters, miners, and many others.

All these men began to gather together at Portsmouth in the beginning of October. The great lords came ready to serve without pay in this war. They were a noble assembly of seven earls, thirty-five barons, and many other gentlemen—all the flower of the English nobility. Thither came the king with all his personal followers. He brought with him thirty falconers on horseback, so that in the intervals of war he might indulge in his favourite pursuit of hawking for water-fowls along the courses of the streams. Besides his falcons, he took with him sixty couples of staghounds, and as many harehounds, that he might hunt when wearied of hawking. Many of the great lords also had their hounds and their falconers with them. Almost every day during the campaign Edward III. and his lords are said to have found time for hunting or hawking.

We can imagine with what feelings Edward, the young Prince of Wales, prepared to start on this his first enterprise. He had been brought up amidst the ideas of chivalry, and regarded war and adventure as the only true vocation of a gentleman. Now at last he was to be allowed to go out into the world himself, and fight the enemy and win his spurs. His father was as enthusiastic as himself. He was then in the flower of his manhood, just thirty-four years old, while the prince was sixteen. They were more like two brothers than father and son.

The destination of the expedition was kept secret. The king's first intention is supposed to have been to sail to Guienne, to aid the Earl of Derby in opposing the French army which had been sent against him. But on board Edward's ship there was a Norman gentleman, Sir Godfrey de Harcourt, who represented to him that Normandy was the richest and most fertile province in France; that it was quite undefended, and that the English would be able to land there without resistance, gain great booty, and subdue many towns before the French army could return from Gascony to oppose them. Edward yielded to his persuasions; and this change of destination shows us that he undertook this expedition without any decided plan. His success was not so much owing to a skilfully arranged campaign as to the personal valour of his troops, and to his own genius as a commander.

The English Army landed at La Hogue on the 10th of July, 1346. It is supposed to have numbered 32,000 men. Edward's first act on landing was to confer knighthood on his son. He found, as Sir Godfrey de Harcourt had said, that his coming was quite unexpected. There was no French army to resist him, and he marched into Normandy without opposition. He divided his troops into three battalions; so arranged they went through the country, pillaging and even burning many of the towns and villages on their way. The fleet meanwhile burnt such ships as it found in the harbours. The rules of chivalry were not concerned with the treatment which a peasant or burgher might receive from the hands of a knight. A knight was bound to treat his equal with courtesy, but his refinement was only one-sided; to the low-born he acknowledged no duties. The chivalrous army of Edward III. spread devastation on every side of the rich and fertile province of Normandy.

At Caen they found a garrison which attempted in vain to defend the town. It was one of the richest towns in Europe, full, as Froissart tells us, "of draperies and all sorts of merchandise, of rich citizens, noble dames and damsels, and fine churches." All its wealth fell into the hands of the English. They stayed in the city for three days, and the plunder they collected was sent down the river in barges to the fleet. The ships were laden with cloths, jewels, gold and silver plate, and merchandise of all kinds. Edward sent orders for all this wealth to be convoyed to England, together with a number of prisoners.

The resistance of Caen had been in vain, and the other cities opened their gates at once to the English. At Louviers, a rich mercantile city, they again won great wealth. Meanwhile Philip had heard of Edward's landing in Normandy, and was hastening to meet him. Edward's intention was to cross the Seine at Rouen, and advance northwards to meet his Flemish allies, who had crossed the frontier. But at Rouen he found the bridge broken down by the French, who, having as yet collected no regular army wherewith to confront him, wished at least to prevent him from crossing the river. Edward continued his march up the left bank of the Seine, hoping to find someplace where he could cross; but all the bridges were broken down. His situation was becoming critical; retreat was impossible, as he had devastated all the country through which he had passed, and he had no supplies to fall back upon.

His one desire was to draw Philip into battle. Philip, on the other hand, wished to gain time; for time reduced the power of Edward, but brought new levies daily to Philip. So Edward continued his course of devastation to Poissy, almost under the walls of Paris. The French peasants, driven from their burning homes, and seeing all their goods carried off by the English soldiers, cried out in despair, "Where is Philip our king?"

It was August when Edward reached Poissy. Philip was encamped with a large army at St. Denis; but Edward failed to draw him out to battle, and did not venture to attack him. The English found the beams of the bridge at Poissy still floating in the river, and Edward determined to wait here whilst his workmen repaired the bridge. He stayed five days in the nunnery at Poissy, where he celebrated the feast of the Assumption of the Virgin Mary, and sat at table in his scarlet robes, trimmed with fur and ermine. When the bridge was rebuilt, the English army crossed the river on the 16th August, dispersing the French on the opposite side with showers of arrows, and marched towards the Somme. They passed the city of Beauvais, but Edward did not venture to stop and besiege it. His army was beginning to diminish. The men suffered from the heat and the rapid marches. They subsisted only on plunder, as they had no supplies with them. Their boots even were beginning to wear out, and there was no means of replacing them. Philip was in their rear with a force greatly superior in numbers. Edward contented himself with burning the suburbs of Beauvais, and passed on towards the Somme.

At Airaines he stopped three days, whilst the Earl of Warwick and Sir Godfrey de Harcourt looked for a place where they might pass the river; but they found all the bridges strongly defended by French troops, and returned in despair to Edward. Philip was now close at hand at Amiens, and the English, hemmed in between the great French army and the river, were thus without way of escape. It was necessary at least to leave Airaines. Edward was thoughtful and silent. He ordered mass to be said before sunrise, and the trumpets sounded for marching. At ten the English left Airaines, and at noon the French entered the town. They found it full of provisions left by the English; the meat was still on the spits, there was bread in the ovens, wine in barrels, and even tables laid ready for dinner. Here the French took up their quarters. The English meanwhile had taken the little town of Oisemont, and established themselves there for the night. Edward caused some prisoners who had been captured on the march to be brought before him, and promised that if any one of them would show him a ford in the river, by which the English army might pass over, he and twenty of his companions should have their liberty.

A peasant, Gobin Agace by name, stood forth, and said he knew of a ford where, when the tide was low, the army might cross in safety; for then the water was only knee-deep, and the bottom was made of gravel and white stones, so that the carriages might pass over without danger. This ford was called Blanquetaque, and was defended by Sir Godemar du Fay with 4,000 men. On the morning of the 24th August, the English waited eagerly for the tide to go out. On the opposite side, the forces of Sir Godemar du Fay were drawn up to defend the ford. Edward gave the word of command in the name of God and St. George, and the English knights plunged into the stream.

The French met them in the water, and desperate deeds of valour were done by the knights on either side as they struggled in the river. Meanwhile, the archers on the banks did much havoc with their persistent showers of arrows. At last the French broke and fled. The English army crossed in safety; but the last of their troops had hardly reached the opposite bank when the light cavalry, who formed the advance guard of the French army, arrived, and succeeded in capturing some loiterers. When Philip himself reached the river the tide had risen, and the ford was impassable. He had to retire to Abbeville, and cross by the bridge there.

The English Army marched on into Ponthieu, and took up their position on the hills near the little village of Cressy. Here Edward determined to halt, and await in an advantageous position the coming of the French. He determined to hazard all on the result of one engagement, though his forces were greatly inferior to the French. Even then, Philip was awaiting at Abbeville the arrival of new troops. But this delay was really advantageous to Edward, as it gave him time to recruit his weary troops, and to make preparations for battle. He had chosen his position with consummate skill. The army was encamped on the rising ground on the right bank of the little River Maye, in front of the town of Cressy. The left wing was protected by the river; in front of it palisades had been erected, and the baggage had been piled together to cover the troops. The right wing was protected by a little wood. The front of the army commanded a ravine on a gentle slope, called la Vallée des Clercs. This arrangement prevented the French from using their cavalry with success, except against the right wing of the English Army.

On the evening of Friday, the 25th August, the soldiers were busy furbishing and mending their armour, so as to be quite ready for the battle. The king gave a great supper to all the earls and barons of the army. They feasted with great cheer, not discouraged by the thought that on the morrow they would have to fight against terrible odds. When his guests had left him, the king retired to his oratory, and kneeling down, prayed to God "that if he should combat his enemies on the morrow, he might come off with honour." It was midnight before he lay down to sleep.

Early the next morning the king and his son heard mass and communicated; the greater part of the army confessed, and did the same. Then the king ordered the men to arm and assemble. He divided his army into three battalions. The first battalion was under the command of the Prince of Wales, who was aided by the Earls of Warwick and Northampton. Stationed in its front was a large body of archers, arranged in the form of a harrow. Behind it, a little to its flank, stood the second battalion, commanded by the Earl of Arundel. The king commanded the third battalion, which formed the reserve, and was stationed on the summit of the hill behind.

When all was arranged, the king mounted a white palfrey, and carrying a white wand in his hand, surrounded by his marshals, rode through the ranks, encouraging the men, and bidding them guard his honour and defend his right. Froissart says:

> He spoke to them so sweetly, and with such cheerful countenance, that all who had been dispirited were directly comforted by seeing and hearing him.

He bade them eat and drink, that they might be strong and vigorous in fighting. There was no hurry or anxiety. When they had eaten, they packed up their pots and barrels in the carts, and put everything in order. Then each man going to his post seated himself on the ground, with his helmet and bow before him, that he might be fresh when the enemy arrived. All the knights had dismounted, intending to fight on foot.

The French had left Abbeville at sunrise. The army, made unwieldy by its size, was weary and disorganised by the long march. The lords who had been sent forward to reconnoitre, came back and advised the French king to let his men rest that night, and not engage battle till the morrow. But the French knights, in proud confidence of their own superiority, were impatient to fight. They pressed forward in a disorderly mass, and when King Philip caught sight of the English his blood began to boil, and he ordered the Genoese archers to form. Just then a fearful thunderstorm swept over the country; the rain fell in torrents; and large flights of crows, startled by the storm, hovered

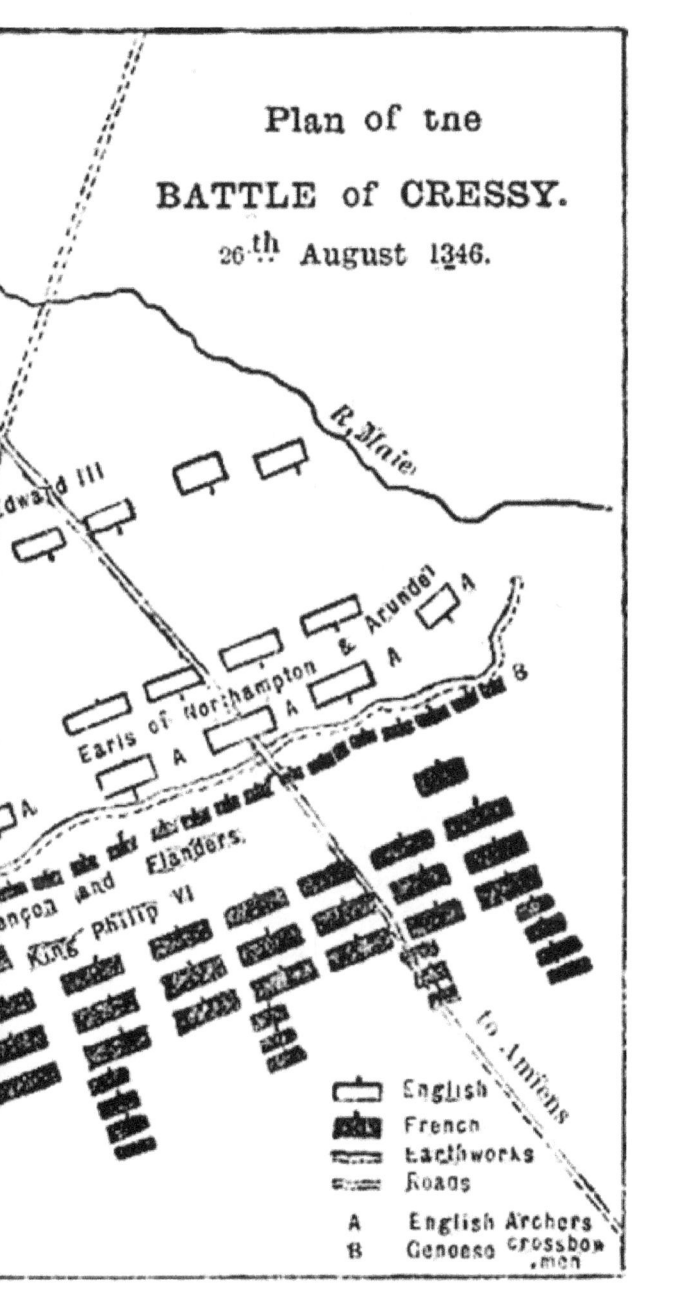

over the French Army, and seemed birds of ill-omen in the eyes of the soldiers. After the storm the sun shone out brightly, and shining in the eyes of the French, dazzled them by its brilliancy; but the English had it at their backs. The rain also had wetted the strings of the Genoese cross-bow men, and by slackening them made it difficult to shoot; but the English kept their long bows in canvas cases, and so they were not harmed by the rain.

The English soldiers were seated on the ground awaiting the approach of the enemy. When the French came in view, the trumpets sounded the note of alarm, and the men sprang to their feet and seized their arms. Evening was drawing on when the two armies met face to face; for it was not till five o'clock that the French army drew near to Cressy. When the Genoese had formed, they advanced with a loud shout, hoping to frighten the English, who stood still and neither moved nor shouted. Then the Genoese set up a second cry, and again a third; but still the same immovable silence on the part of the English was maintained. Only when they presented their cross-bows, and began to shoot, did the English answer; then their answer was a shower of arrows, poured with such force and quickness that it seemed as if it snowed.

The Genoese threw down their arms in terror, and tried to seek safety in flight. The Duke of Alençon, who was commanding the French battalion in the rear, enraged at seeing them fly, shouted to his men, "Kill me these scoundrels, for they stop up our road without any reason." The French men-at-arms pressed on through the flying Genoese, killing all who came in their way. But the shower of English arrows never ceased. With sure and steady aim the archers penetrated into the French ranks. Together with Alençon advanced the blind King of Bohemia, who rode between two knights, to whose bridles he had caused his horse to be fastened, that they might lead him into the thickest of the fray.

And now the time was come for the English knights to meet the French. Prince Edward, followed by his knights, sprang forward from behind the ranks of his archers, and rushed upon Alençon and his followers. Then ensued a terrible *mêlée*. Knight struggled with knight in hand to hand combat. The prince's Welsh foot-soldiers made great havoc amongst the French with their short knives. Over all fell a ceaseless shower of arrows from the unshaken ranks of the English archers. The second battalion of the English Army came to the aid of the first. The numbers of the French seemed so overwhelming, that a knight was sent in great haste to the King of England, who was still posted with his reserve near the windmill on the hill. He begged the king to come to the prince's assistance.

"Is my son dead," asked the king, "unhorsed, or so badly wounded that he cannot support himself?"

"Nay, thank God," answered the knight, "but he is in so hot an engagement that he has great need of your help."

The king only said, "Let the boy win his spurs; for I am determined, if it please God, that all the glory and honour of this day shall be given to him, and to those into whose care I have entrusted him."

Truly the young prince won his spurs. He and his knights fought with such desperate valour that soon the French began to break in disorder, though not before many of their bravest knights had been slain on the field. It is said that 1,600 barons, 4,000 esquires, and 20,000 common soldiers fell on the French side; whilst the English loss was inconsiderable. It was a ghastly scene upon which the moon shone down that night. On all sides the French were flying. Some knights and squires still wandered over the field amongst the dead and dying, seeking their masters whom they had lost. They attacked the English in small parties, but were soon destroyed; for no quarter was given that day. Late in the evening Sir John Hainault led King Philip from the field by force. The king fled through the night to Amiens, and then on to Paris.

The English were left victors on the field. King Edward came down from his post, and hastened to his son. Kissing him with enthusiasm, he said, "My fair son, God Almighty give you grace to persevere as you have begun." A deep mist rose, and the battlefield was enveloped in the blackest darkness. The English only knew that their enemies had fled by the silence which had succeeded the hooting and shouting of the French. Pursuit was impossible in the darkness. They kindled great fires and lit torches, which shed a weird light on the battlefield. The battle had lasted from five o'clock on Saturday evening till two o'clock on Sunday morning. The night passed quietly; for all rioting had been forbidden. When morning dawned, Edward gave orders that the mass of the Holy Ghost should be solemnly sung by the soldiers in thanksgiving for this great victory. The thick mist still continued. Two bodies of French soldiers, who came upon the field ignorant of the battle, and hoping to join the French army, were entirely routed by the English, and many of them were slain.

Edward III. remained two days upon the field of battle, to superintend the numbering and burial of the dead. He granted a truce for three days, that the peasantry might come and aid in the task. "What think you of a battle," said Edward to his son, as they wandered over the field, "is it a pleasant game?" Orders were given to attend to the wounded, some of whom were given shelter by the monks of a neighbouring abbey. The bodies of the dead nobles were taken to be buried in the surrounding churches, mostly in the church at Cressy. The body of the blind King of Bohemia was sent away to Luxembourg, to be buried by his son. For the burial of the common soldiers the peasants dug long, deep ditches, traces of which may be seen to this day.

So was won the Battle of Cressy, the first of England's great series of victories upon the continent. It showed the powerlessness of chivalry before the strength of the people. The proudest knights of France had fallen helpless before the English yeoman, with his bow and arrows. It showed that the strength of a nation no longer lay in the brilliant appearance or the boasted bravery of its knights, but in the steadfastness and sturdy courage of its people. The death-knell of chivalry was sounded. Its pomp and pageantry might still continue for awhile, and meet with encouragement from Edward III.; but he was wise enough to recognise the truth, and know that it was to his archers, and not to his knights, that he owed this victory. Cressy was not only a triumph of the English over the French; it was a triumph of the people over the nobles.

Chapter 4

The Siege of Calais

After the Battle of Cressy, the road to Calais lay open to Edward III. It was of the utmost importance to him to gain possession of this town. Its port was the home of the French pirates who so fatally damaged his commerce. If he could but gain possession of it, they would be destroyed, and he would gain a new and convenient harbour for his trade with Flanders.

To take Calais by assault was hopeless on account of its strong fortifications. Edward determined to besiege it, and reduce the town by starvation. He caused to be built round its walls a whole town of wooden houses, in which he lodged his army. This wooden town was laid out in streets, and the houses were thatched with straw. There was even a market-place, where markets were held on Wednesdays and Saturdays. English and Flemish merchants brought cloth, bread and meat, and supplies of all kinds for the comfort of the army. Communications were opened with England, and money was asked for and obtained from Parliament. English ships blockaded the harbour, and were stationed all along the coast so as to cut off all approach to the unfortunate city. Reinforcements came over from England. Queen Philippa joined her husband in the camp. The English waited patiently in confidence of success.

The English arms were successful on all sides. The French withdrew from the Garonne, and left the English in undisputed possession of Guienne and Poitou. But in England itself a great danger had arisen. The Scots were always ready and eager to cross the border. Now that they knew that the King of England was away in France with all his bravest soldiers, they thought that there would be no one to resist them, and that they would be able to march unopposed to the gates of London itself. A large army under David Bruce crossed the border and proceeded as far as Durham, burning and destroying everything in their way. But the Archbishop of York and the Lords Henry Percy and Ralph Nevil had gathered together all the men they could find, amongst whom were even many clergymen, eager to fight in defence of their country. They came upon the Scots unawares at Nevil's Cross, near Durham. The English fought valiantly, wishing to emulate their victorious countrymen at Cressy. Here again the English archers decided the day. The Scots were completely routed. David Bruce, the great Earl Douglas, and many other nobles, were taken prisoners, whilst still more lay lifeless on the field. David Bruce was taken to London, which he entered solemnly, riding upon a horse, amidst a great concourse of spectators, who received him with silent respect. He was led to the Tower, where he was destined to remain a long while.

In Britany also the English arms had been successful. Charles of Blois, de Montfort's rival, had been taken prisoner, and was sent to the Tower. The King of France was determined at least to save Calais. Messages were sent to him by John of Vienne, the governor of Calais, saying that he could not hold out much longer. Seventeen hundred of the useless inhabitants of the town had already been turned out, and had been kindly received by the English, who gave them food and suffered them to pass on. The garrison had eaten all the dogs and cats in the town; starvation was staring them in the face; they must surrender if help did not come. Philip assembled an army at Whitsuntide, and marched to raise the siege of the suffering city. But when he drew near he found that it was impossible to approach the English army, which was securely entrenched. He sent messengers to Edward asking him to come out and give him battle in the open field. But, afraid to risk another battle after the defeat of Cressy, he determined to leave the city to its fate, and broke up his camp. The unfortunate garrison saw the army, which they had hoped would save them, turn its back without striking a blow.

Further resistance was hopeless, and the famished garrison asked for terms. Edward would grant none. He was enraged with the city on account of its obstinacy, and hated its citizens because of the many deeds of piracy by which they had injured his commerce. He sent Sir Walter Manny to the governor, saying that he would grant mercy to the garrison and the inhabitants, if six of the principal *burghers* gave themselves unconditionally into his hands, with ropes round their necks, and the keys of the town in their hands.

When the governor had heard the king's answer from Sir Walter Manny, he went into the market-place, and caused the bell to be rung. When all the inhabitants of the town had assembled, he told them what the King of England had said. Then there was great weeping and lamentation, till up rose the wealthiest citizen of the town, Eustace de St. Pierre, and said, "It would be a very great pity to suffer so many people to die through famine. I will be the first of the six." Then the citizens seemed as though they would have worshipped him, falling at his feet with tears and groans. It was not long before others were found willing to die for their fellow-citizens. They were followed to the gates by lamentations, and Sir Walter Manny led them to the king's pavilion. There they fell upon their knees before Edward, and presenting him with the keys, begged him to have mercy upon them. So pitiful was the sight that the English barons and knights who stood around wept to behold it.

Edward only eyed them angrily; for he hated the citizens of Calais. Then spoke Sir Walter Manny: "Ah, gentle king, restrain your anger; let not the world have cause to speak ill of you for your cruelty." But Edward refused to listen.

Queen Philippa threw herself on her knees before him, and said with tears, "Ah, gentle sir, since I have crossed the seas with great danger to see you, I have never asked you one favour; now I most humbly ask as a gift, for the sake of the Son of the blessed Mary, and for your love to me, that you will be merciful to these men."

The king, after looking at her in silence for some time, said, "Ah, lady, I wish you had been otherwhere; but I cannot refuse you; I give them to you to do as you please." Then the queen and all the knights were very joyful, and Philippa took the noble citizens to her tent, and gave them new clothing and feasted them, and giving them each six nobles of gold, sent them out of the camp in safety.

It was on the 4th August that Calais fell into the hands of the English. Edward caused all its inhabitants to leave it, except some few who made their peace by swearing fealty to him. To re-people the town, he offered great privileges to such English merchants as would settle there. Soon it became again a bustling, busy, commercial city, and was of great importance to the trade of England during the 211 years that it remained in her possession.

Edward stayed some little while at Calais, during which time Prince Edward led frequent foraging expeditions into France. Pope Clement VI. had been unceasing in his attempts to make peace between the Kings of France and England. Now once more his legates appeared upon the scene, and at last succeeded in negotiating a truce, which was agreed upon on the 28th September, and was to last till a fortnight after the next Midsummer-day.

On the 12th October, the king and his son landed at Sandwich. This time he did not return without having done something decisive. Between the 10th July, 1346, and the 4th August, 1347, the great battles of Cressy and Nevil's Cross had been won, and Calais had been taken. The Tower was crowded with noble prisoners; the whole country was enriched by the spoil won from the French. All this showed the power of the English people, the ability of their king, and the bravery of his son. It was a proud moment for England when her king and his son came home, crowned with the laurels of victory. After this Edward stayed almost constantly in England, and devoted himself to domestic legislation, as he had entire confidence in the ability of his son to conduct foreign campaigns. It is supposed that Prince Edward gained the name of the Black Prince from the French, after the Battle of Cressy, when he fought in a black *cuirass*.

Sometime after the siege of Calais Edward III. left England once again, to indulge in an adventure which was more befitting a knight-errant than a king. He heard that Geoffroy de Chargny, a French knight, had been trying to bribe the Genoese commander whom he had left in charge of Calais. Edward gave orders that the negotiations should be continued, and arrangements made to admit a body of French soldiers, under Geoffroy de Chargny, at the great gate of Calais leading to Boulogne. He then crossed the seas with his son, Sir Walter Manny, and a picked body of knights. The king and his son were to fight disguised under the banner of Sir Walter Manny.

At the hour appointed the great gates were opened, and the French were preparing to enter, when the English sprang from their ambuscade, and with shouts of "Manny to the rescue," fell upon the French. Sir Geoffroy saw that he had been betrayed; but turning to his men, he said, "Gentlemen, if we fly we shall lose all; let us fight valiantly, in the hope that the day may be ours." Then there were many stout passages of arms between the English and the French. The King of England singled out the bravest knight among the French, Sir Eustace de Ribeaumont, who had no idea with whom he fought, and twice struck Edward down on his knees. At last he was obliged to surrender himself to the king, and the honour of the day belonged to the English. All the French were either slain or captured.

Only after the fight did the French know that the King of England had been there in person. It was the evening of the New Year, and Edward determined to celebrate the night with a great feast, to which the French prisoners were bidden. All were seated round the table with the king, dressed in new robes. All, English and French alike, made good cheer. Prince Edward and the English knights served up the first course, and waited on their guests, then seated themselves quietly at another table. After supper the tables were removed, and the king remained in the hall talking with the knights. To Sir Eustace de Ribeaumont he said, smiling:

> Sir Eustace, you are the most valiant knight in Christendom that I ever saw attack his enemy or defend himself. I never yet found any one in battle who, hand to hand, gave me so much to do as you have done this day. I adjudge to you, as your just due, the prize of valour above all the knights of my court.

The king then took off a chaplet of pearls, very rich and handsome, which he wore round his head, and placed it upon the head of Sir Eustace, bidding him wear it for love of him. He also gave him his liberty, without ransom, allowing him to go on the morrow wherever he would.

CHAPTER 5

Chivalry

The victories in France had brought great wealth and prosperity into England. The booty won from France was spread throughout the land, and the matrons of England clothed themselves in the garments of the matrons of France. The result was not altogether beneficial. This increased wealth brought with it also a change in the simplicity of English manners. Wearing the more extravagant dress of the French, sleeping on their feather beds, clothing themselves in their rich furs, the people's taste grew more extravagant. They acquired a love for fine clothes, for foolish fashions and foppery of all kinds; and in this extravagance the clergy rivalled the laity. There was also an increased love of pageantry and dissipation, in which the people were encouraged by the king.

Tournaments were so frequent that Edward had to pass an enactment forbidding them to be held without royal permission. Yet he himself caused nineteen to be held between October, 1347, and May, 1348, many of which lasted more than a fortnight. The life of the court, and of the nobles, was nothing but a ceaseless round of gaieties and festivities. It was at one of these tournaments that Edward III. established the great Order of the Garter, which continues to this day, and may be looked upon as a heritage left to us by the chivalric spirit of the Middle Ages.

Chivalry was a thing of French creation, and throve naturally on French soil. It is principally the French and Provençal *troubadours* who have celebrated it by their song. In England it never developed so freely. It seemed like a thing imported, foreign in its very nature to English simplicity and English bluntness. Still throughout the Middle Ages the chivalric spirit ruled supreme all over Europe, in England and France alike. When chivalry ceased to be an enthusiasm it became a fashion, and lingered on as a fashion till Cervantes heaped ridicule upon it in his *Don Quixote*; till its absurdities became so manifest that it faded away amid the scorn and laughter of mankind. Edward III. aimed at being a type of fashionable knighthood. In his day chivalry had not yet become an absurdity. It had lost much of its early simplicity and elevation, but still in the Black Prince and some of his knights, such as Sir John Chandos, Sir Walter Manny, and Sir James Audeley, we find all the nobleness and greatness of early chivalry.

Let us look a little closer at this chivalry, and see what it meant and what was the ideal which it held up to its followers. It had no artificial origin, but sprang up as a natural outcome of feudalism, and so of early Teutonic manners. A feudal vassal owed certain definite duties to his superior. Knighthood was the formal act by which the fitness of a young man to take upon him these duties was recognised, and he was declared worthy to enter the rank of warriors.

It was to the Crusades that chivalry owed its religious character. By taking part in the Crusades the knight could best find a field in which he might give free play to all the noble sentiments which animated him. And if the knight was to fight for Christ, it was right that religion should take under her control the important act which initiated a young man into the rank of knighthood. The education of a future knight began at the age of seven. It was the custom for the sons of gentlemen to be brought up in the castles of the nobles, where first they acted as pages, attending upon the lords and ladies. Afterwards they were advanced, at the age of fourteen, to the rank of squires, and waited upon their lords both at home and abroad; they aided in their toilet, carved before them at table, and riveted their armour as they attended them to the tournament or the battle.

Attention was paid to their education in all things connected with the management of arms or of horses; they were taught above all to be courteous to ladies, to be respectful and obedient to their superiors. Thus bred up in the atmosphere of chivalry, they were fit and eager, when manhood came, to be raised to the dignity of knighthood. This was accompanied by many solemn ceremonies. The squire who was to be knighted was first made to lay aside his clothes, and enter a bath, the symbol of purification. On coming out he was clothed with a white garment, the symbol of purity; next, in a red robe, the symbol of the blood he was bound to shed in the service of the faith; and lastly, in a close black coat, the symbol of the death which awaited him. He then spent the next twenty-four hours in fasting. At evening he entered the church or chapel, and passed the night in prayers. In the morning he confessed and received absolution, and then partook of the Communion.

He was next present at the mass of the Holy Ghost, and sometimes listened to a sermon on the duties of knighthood. Then, advancing to the altar, with the sword of a knight hanging from his neck, he knelt before the priest, who took the sword and blessed it, and then returned it to him. After this he went and knelt before the noble who was to arm him knight, who was called his godfather. Before him he swore to maintain the right, to fight for the faith, to serve his sovereign prince, to protect the weak and oppressed; above all, to be the champion of women, to obey his superiors, to honour his companions, to keep faith with all the world, to forswear all treason and avarice, to acknowledge as his only aims glory and virtue. When he had taken his oath, knights and ladies advanced to clothe him in his new armour, the spurs, the coat of mail, the cuirass, and the gauntlets, and to gird on his sword. Then his godfather struck him three blows with the flat of his sword, saying, "In the name of God, of Saint Michael, and of Saint George, I dub thee knight."

The young knight then seized his helmet, and sprang upon his horse, brandishing his lance, and rode out to show himself to the crowd outside the church. There was always great feasting and joy when the eldest son was knighted. His father gathered round him all his vassals, who owed him a money contribution on this joyful occasion. They feasted together in the great hall of the castle. The lord himself was seated at the high table on the dais at one end of the hall, but with his face turned towards the hall, that all might see him. During the feast the guests were entertained with the performances of jesters, tumblers, and jugglers, who formed part of all the great households of that time; or they listened to the romances of the troubadours.

So amidst general rejoicings the young man entered on his new career. The ideal of perfect knighthood held before him was noble and exalted, and we cannot doubt but that it fired him with enthusiasm, and inspired him to do noble deeds. In an age of rough and rude manners, when the majority of men were wanting in all refinement and culture, when men for the most part were animated only by low and selfish aims, when the light shed around by religion was as yet only feeble and fitful, it was a great thing to have such an ideal as this held up before men. In the Crusades the knight found his true field. By them the use of the sword was sanctified, and the warrior could find joy in feats of arms whilst fighting for Christ. And as the Crusades sanctified the warlike feats of the knight, his worship of the Virgin sanctified that devotion to the ladies which was so distinguishing a feature of chivalry. "*God and the ladies,*" was the motto of every true knight.

He went both to tournament and to battle with his lady's badge upon his arm, and thoughts of her nerved him to deeds of valour. His honour was the dearest thing in a knight's eyes, and from this sprung his scrupulous fidelity to his word once pledged. As a lover, he must be faithful to the lady he served; as a vassal, he must be faithful to his lord; a promise once given, even to an enemy, must never be broken. During the French wars of Edward III. we hear often of knights being released on their word, to raise the money required for their ransom, and returning of their own accord to captivity if they could not raise this money.

Courtesy was another distinguishing feature of chivalry. By this was meant true courtesy, springing from the heart, and showing itself in modesty, consideration for others, self-denial, as well as in matters of outward gesture and punctilio. Courtesy was shown as much to foe as to friend, and did much towards softening the ferocity of war. A true knight must also be liberal; he must be inspired with an active sense of justice, and a burning indignation of wrong. But whilst extending the sympathy of a knight to all his companions in knighthood, whether friend or foe, chivalry narrowed his sympathy to those of his own class. Princes did their utmost to encourage chivalry, to provide tournaments where their knights might exhibit their valour, and to cover them with every possible distinction.

But while caring for the knights they forgot the people. The spirit of chivalry was a class spirit, and narrowing in its tendency. It recognised neither the rights nor the interests of the people; and when once the people had grown strong enough to assert their rights, and make their importance felt, the doom of chivalry was sealed. It continued to exist with all its pageantry long after its real life and spirit was dead. Perhaps it was never so magnificent in its outward show as it was during the reign of Edward III., when its decay had already begun.

Never had there been so many and such splendid tournaments at the English court as now after the battle of Cressy. It is uncertain at which of these Edward founded the order of the Garter; but it is known to have been in existence in 1348. Most probably it was founded at the great tournament, held at Eltham in 1347. Ever since

1344, when Edward had made a Round Table at Windsor in imitation of the traditional Round Table of King Arthur, he had been desirous of establishing a new order of knighthood. This desire was ripened into fulfilment by the prosperous condition of the country after the battle of Cressy. A trivial incident decided the motto and badge which he should adopt for the new order. One of the ladies of the court, by some supposed to be Queen Philippa herself, by others, the Countess of Salisbury, dropped her garter. Whilst the courtiers looked at one another and smiled, shrugging their shoulders as they pointed to the garter on the floor, Edward with the gallantry of a true knight picked it up, and handing it to the lady, said, "*Honi soit qui mal y pense.*" ("Shame to him who thinks evil.") As he did so, the thought flashed through his mind that here were the badge and the motto for his new Order.

The Order was established with great pomp and ceremony. St. George was instituted as its patron saint. A chapel to St. George was ordered to be built at Windsor, as chapel for the Order. There each of the twenty-five knights, who were to be honoured with the garter, was to have his appointed stall, over which during his lifetime his helmet and sword were to hang. There all the knights were to assemble, if it were in any way possible, on the eve of St. George's-day. Then, sitting each in his stall, they were to hear mass. On St. George's-day itself, a great tournament and banquet was to be held; on the day following a requiem was to be sung for the souls of the faithful deceased.

No knight of the Order was ever to pass near Windsor without coming to the chapel, and there was to put on his mantle and hear mass. Edward made a foundation at the chapel of thirteen secular canons and thirteen vicars, and also of twenty-six veteran knights, who were to be maintained there, and were to serve God continually in prayer. The kings of England were to be perpetual sovereigns of the Order. There were twenty-five knights-founders, amongst whom was, of course, the Black Prince, with his principal knights, Chandos, Sir James Audley and the Captale de Buche. They were nearly all young men; four of them were even under twenty, and ten under thirty; Edward III. himself was only thirty-five.

At the first feast we read that all these founders, together with the king, were clothed in gowns of russet, powdered with blue garters, wearing like garters also on their right legs, and mantles of blue, with escutcheons of St. George. Bareheaded, and in this apparel, they heard mass, which was celebrated by Simon Islip, Archbishop of Canterbury, and afterwards went to the feast, setting themselves orderly at the table.

Then followed splendid tournaments, at which there were two kinds of conflicts. In the tournaments proper the knights divided themselves into parties, and one party fought against another. There were also jousts, or conflicts between two knights. These were generally held in honour of the ladies, who presided as judges over them. The combatants used spears without heads of iron; their object was to strike their opponent upon the front of his helmet, so as to beat him backwards upon his horse, or else to break his spear.

Though the tournaments were only looked upon as sport, they were often attended with great danger, and the knights engaged in the combat were not seldom severely wounded, and even killed. But no thought of this danger, incurred for no good reason, diminished in the least the enthusiasm for them. They were attended with every possible kind of magnificence. The lists within which the combatants were to fight were superbly decorated, and were surrounded by pavilions belonging to the champions, and ornamented with their arms and banners. Scaffolds were erected for the noble spectators, both lords and ladies; those upon which the royal family sat were hung with tapestry and embroideries of gold and silver. Every spectator was decked in the most sumptuous manner.

Not only the knights themselves, but their horses, their pages, and the heralds, were clothed in costly and glittering apparel. The clanging of trumpets, the shouts of the beholders, the cries of the heralds increased the excitement of the fray. When the tournament was over, the combatants retired to their pavilions to refresh themselves after the fight and remove their heavy armour, the weight of which was almost unbearable. In the evening they met together with the nobles and ladies who had been spectators of the sport, and the time was passed in feasting, dancing, and singing. The heralds named those who had fought best on both sides. The ladies chose a name for each party, and the champions received the rewards of their merit from the hands of two young and noble maidens.

Children were taught from their earliest childhood to relish these spectacles; their very toys were made in imitation of knights jousting. The number of these tournaments led to very great extravagance in dress. Each person wished to excel his neighbour in the magnificence of his attire. The great desire was to appear in something new and astounding, and this led to the most fantastic fashions. Ladies of the first rank and greatest beauty might be seen on these occasions dressed in parti-coloured tunics, half one colour and half another, with handsomely ornamented girdles of gold and silver, in which were stuck short swords or daggers. In this masculine attire they appeared mounted on the finest horses they could procure, ornamented with the richest furniture. Parti-coloured garments were in great favour. Men would wear one stocking of one colour, the other of another. Most noticeable among the many extravagant fashions were the trailing dresses, which lay in heaps upon the ground, in front as well as behind; the long and fantastically shaped sleeves trailed also on the ground. A contemporary writer says:

> The tailors must soon shape their garments in the open field, for want of room to cut them in their own houses; because that man is best respected who bears upon his back at one time the greatest quantity of cloth and of fur.

Edward III. himself set the example in these extravagant fashions. In his wardrobe-rolls we find accounts of dresses which were to be worn at tournaments. One was a tunic and a cloak with a hood, on which were to be embroidered one hundred garters, with buckles, bars, and pendants of silver; also a doublet of linen, having round the skirts and about the sleeves a deep border of green cloth, worked with representations of clouds with vine branches of gold, and this motto, given by the king, "*It is as it is.*" The festival of the Garter was celebrated with great splendour in 1351. The king wore a robe of cloth of gold furred, another of red velvet embroidered with clouds and eagles of pearl and gold, each eagle having in his beak a garter with the motto of the order. The queen wore a similar robe, and the Princess Isabel wore a red velvet robe, embroidered with 119 circles of silk and pearls, with trees of silk and gold embroidered on a ground of green velvet, with flowers and leaves. On another occasion we read that a grant of £200 (equal to £3,000 of our money—*as at time of first publication*) was made to Queen Philippa for her attire at a festival of the Garter.

These gorgeous robes were of course exceedingly valuable, and were reckoned amongst the most important possessions of the great people. The Black Prince disposed by will of the chief of his robes, describing them each separately. Another way in which the royal family and the nobility displayed their grandeur was by their magnificent bedhangings. Of these again the Black Prince disposed by will. He seems to have possessed many different beds with gorgeous hangings: one set of hangings was embroidered with mermaids, another with swans, and so on. Gold and silver plate was another favourite article of luxury. The city of London made several very handsome presents of large quantities of plate both to the king and to the prince.

But amidst all this apparent luxury we must not forget the other side of the picture, the squalor and discomfort in which even the greatest people lived in those days. Glazed windows were only just beginning to be used. The walls of the rooms were commonly bare, and only on grand occasions were covered with hangings. The Black Prince, we know, possessed some splendid hangings. One set was embroidered with swans having ladies' heads, and another was embroidered with eagles and griffins. These he used to carry about with him to ornament his hall on great occasions.

The floors were covered with rushes, and were the receptacles of all kinds of filth. Bones were thrown at dinner on the floor for the dogs, who were beneath the table ready to devour them. Forks were not known, and the food was mostly torn in pieces with the fingers. Wooden platters were largely in use, or more often a large slice of bread, on which each man would lay his portion of meat. At banquets, a lady and knight used to eat off the same plate. There were only two meals in the course of the day—dinner, which took place between ten and eleven, and supper at five o'clock. The entire household dined together in the same hall. The chief ornament of the dinner-table was a massive saltcellar, and the places for the persons of the greatest dignity were always above the salt. Edward III. possessed among his royal jewels a silver ship, which was used to ornament the dinner-table and hold sweetmeats. Gold and silver ewers were used for washing before and after meat. The great hall, or dining-room, was also the sleeping room for the servants; there were private sleeping rooms for the chief members of the family.

Each great nobleman had around him a number of officers like a royal court—chamberlains, chancellors, and others. Besides these, he kept in his employ companies of minstrels, jugglers, tumblers, and players, who sang and displayed their tricks for the amusement of the company during their meals. Travelling companies of minstrels and jugglers wandered over the country, giving performances in the various noblemen's houses. *Tregetours*, or conjurers, were in high favour. There were both male and female tumblers, who went about together in companies, called gleman's companies; they also amused their audiences with buffoonery of all kinds. Other men made it their profession to train bears, apes, and horses to perform tricks. The spectators always connected these tricks with witchcraft, and supposed them to be done by means of magic.

Theatres did not exist in those days; but there were mysteries or miracle plays, which formed a great part of the amusement of the people during the fourteenth and fifteenth centuries. Their origin was no doubt purely religious, and their object was to illustrate passages of Scripture and teach moral lessons. They were performed in churches, or on stages erected in the churchyards and the fields, and sometimes on movable stages in the streets. They were written by monks, and were performed sometimes by monks themselves, sometimes by the members of a trade-gild. They seem very soon to have lost most of their religious character, and to have become little more than a means of amusement for the people; to secure this better, they degenerated into rather coarse comedies.

Three complete sets of these old mysteries still exist, and in all we see the same desire for comic effect, which led the authors to take liberties with the text of Scripture, so as to be able to introduce comic incidents. Noah's wife is a favourite character, and is endowed with a very obstinate temper, so that Noah has great difficulty in getting her into the ark. Devils played an important part, and were represented with horns, tails, claws, and terrible masks. Everything possible was done to make them awful in the eyes of the women and children. Masks were much used in the performance; the women's parts were acted by men or boys wearing masks. The play as a whole cannot have produced any very serious impression, though it was by no means entirely deficient in religious feeling. But the comic element predominated, and gave rise to the most boisterous merriment. We cannot wonder therefore that the preachers and moralists of the day regarded the miracle plays with disfavour, and spoke of them in the same way as the Puritans of later date did of the theatres.

These mysteries were exhibited on festivals and holidays. Another kind of play, called "*Ludi*," was exhibited at court during the Christmas holidays. These plays were really nothing more than mummeries—the appearance of a large number of persons in masks and various comic dresses, personifying certain characters, and performing dances.

In 1348 Edward III. kept his Christmas at Guildford. Orders were given to manufacture for the Christmas sports eighty tunics of buckram of different colours, and a large number of masks—some with faces of women, some with beards, some like angel heads of silver. There were to be mantles embroidered with heads of dragons, tunics wrought with heads and wings of peacocks, and embroidered in many other fantastic ways. The celebration of Christmas lasted from All-Hallows Eve, the 31st October, till the day after the Purification, the 3rd February. At the court a lord of misrule was appointed, who reigned during the whole of this period, and was called "the master of merry disports." He ruled over and organised all the games and sports, and during the period of his rule there was nothing but a succession of *masques*, disguisings, and dances of all kinds. All the nobles, even the mayor of London, had an officer of this kind chosen in their households. Dancing was a very favourite amusement. It was practised by the nobility of both sexes. The damsels of London spent their evenings in dancing before their masters' doors, and the country lasses danced upon the village green.

The favourite occupation of the nobility was hunting. In the reign of Edward II. hunting had been reduced to a science, and rules had been established for its practice. Edward III. was an ardent hunter, and all the nobility followed his example. Even bishops and abbots hunted. No more valuable present could be made than a harehound or deerhound. In hawking, ladies could also take part. The careful training of a falcon required great skill, and a well-trained bird was most highly prized. Embroidered gloves were worn on the hand upon which the falcon was to sit. When not flying at their game, the hawks used to be hoodwinked with elegant hoods. They had a bell on each leg, and there was a difference of a semitone between the two bells.

The English ladies led a quiet and secluded life, and were celebrated for their skill in needlework and embroidery. They used also to amuse themselves with playing at dice and chess, and with music. They were allowed, it is true, to appear as spectators at the tournaments; and at the time of the foundation of the Order of the Garter, the queen and the wives of the knights-founders were received, as far as their sex allowed, as members of the Order.

CHAPTER 6

The Black Death

The famous Order of the Garter had been established. Men were feasting and carousing, and were spending their days in brilliant festivals, while the shadow of a great calamity was creeping over the land. A terrible plague had broken out in the interior of Asia. It spread rapidly to Europe, devastated Greece and Italy, and passed on through France to England. Its coming is said to have been heralded by the most frightful signs. A stinking mist seemed to advance from the East and spread over Europe. Numerous earthquakes shook the Continent, and meteors of great size were seen. It was in August, 1348, that the plague first reached the shores of England. Three months afterwards it reached London.

We can hardly imagine the terror which the plague must have spread over the country. No one could feel himself safe from its ravages. Before the plague the population of England is supposed to have been 5,000,000; it is calculated that at least 2,500,000 persons perished of it.

The disease seemed to be a poisoning of the blood. It began with shivering, which was followed by a burning internal fever, and then boils of a black colour appeared upon the skin, whence it gained its name the "Black Death." Death often ensued after a few hours' illness. The terror of death only increased the danger, and gave rise to utter selfishness and recklessness. Men deserted those dearest to them when they were stricken by the plague; brothers deserted their sisters, husbands their wives, mothers their children. Some shut themselves up in utter solitude, and hoped, by living moderately and avoiding all contact with men, to escape the danger. Others indulged in the wildest dissipation, and strove to drown their anxiety by reckless drinking, and excitement of all kinds. The mere sight of a stricken person was supposed to be sufficient to communicate infection. No one ventured to walk abroad without bearing in their hands some pungent herb, the smell of which was believed to disinfect the pestilential air.

The rich shut themselves up in their castles, and in many cases succeeded in escaping infection. It was amongst the poor that the mortality was greatest. From the large number of parish priests who are known to have died of the plague, we are led to hope that they at least did not shun the danger, but went boldly amongst the sick and dying to administer the last comforts of religion. We know that seventeen out of twenty-one of the York clergy died during the pestilence. It was in the eastern counties that the mortality was the greatest. They were at that time the most thickly populated part of England. For many years there had been a slow and constant immigration of Flemings, who had been encouraged by the English kings to settle in England, that they might there establish their industries.

From them the English had learnt weaving and commercial enterprise. The east, not the west, of England was then the centre of manufactures and industry. Norwich was a thriving manufacturing city, possessing sixty parish churches and sixteen chapels. There exists a record, stating that 57,374 persons died there of the plague. Norwich never recovered its prosperity. At the present day, (1904), it has only thirty-six parish churches, in place of sixty before 1348. Yarmouth was of great importance as a station for the herring fishery; out of 10,000 inhabitants, it lost 7,000 by the plague. In Bristol, then one of the chief towns in England, the plague raged to such an extent that the living were scarcely able to bury the dead, and grass grew several inches high in the principal streets.

In London its ravages were terrible. The churchyards were filled to overflowing, and no longer sufficed. Sir Walter Manny bought a piece of land in West Smithfield to bury the dead, and built a chapel where masses should be said for the souls of the departed. This was the origin of the Charterhouse. Other persons also bought pieces of land for the same purpose, and fields were set apart where the dead were buried in large pits. Two successive Archbishops of Canterbury died of the plague, John de Ufford, and Thomas Bradwardine, one of the most learned men of his time. One of the king's daughters, the Princess Joan, died of it at Bordeaux, on her way to marry Don Pedro of Castile.

By many people the Black Death was looked upon as a scourge sent by God for the sins of mankind. A sect of fanatics, called the Flagellants, arose and wandered over all parts of Europe. There appeared in London, in 1349, a band of men and women, 120 in number, whose object was to expiate in their own persons the sins of the world. They wandered from town to town clad in sackcloth, with red crosses on their caps, chanting penitential hymns. From time to time they prostrated themselves upon the ground in the form of a cross, and took it in turns for one of their number to scourge their naked backs and shoulders. This process was repeated every morning for thirty-three days, the number of the years of Christ's life upon earth. Then the fanatics, having fulfilled the appointed penance, returned to their own homes, having in many cases inspired others to follow their example. So great was their enthusiasm that they seemed not to feel the stroke of the scourge, and sang their wild hymns only with greater exultation as the blood streamed from their shoulders. The following is a translation of a verse of one of their hymns:

Through love of man the Saviour came,
Through love of man He died;
He suffered want, reproach, and shame,
Was scourged and crucified.
Oh think, then, on thy Saviour's pain,
And lash the sinner, lash again!

In England they found no response to their enthusiasm. The people only gazed and wondered, and they departed without having gained any followers. In Germany their success was much greater.

The result of the Black Death in England was a social revolution, which changed the whole course of English history. It disturbed the existing relations of land and labour, by increasing suddenly the value of labour whilst it diminished the value of land. We cannot follow in detail the course of this revolution, but we can trace some of the causes which produced it. So large a number of the labourers had died of the plague, that there were none left to till the land. Flocks and herds wandered over the country with no one to tend them. The labourers, being few in number, demanded wages which the farmers were not able to pay and make a profit.

Land consequently fell in value, and it became possible for one man to hold a large quantity of it. The small farms were broken up, as it was easier for a small farmer to gain his livelihood by working for another man than by attempting to get others to work for him, and make a profit out of his own land. Arable land was largely converted into pasture land, because pasture land required fewer labourers.

The immediate consequence of the plague was the outbreak of the first great conflict in the history of England between capital and labour. The free labourer at that time can hardly be said to have had a position recognised by law. According to the system of land tenure which had prevailed in England since its colonization by German tribes, the serf was bound to the land. He was not a slave in the sense that he could be bought or sold; but he was his lord's property, for he could not move from the soil on which he had been born: he was an outlaw if he attempted to leave it without his lord's permission. As time went on the serf had gained certain rights. The amount of service due by him to his lord had been limited by custom; he had a legal right to the piece of land on which his hut was built; the labour which he owed to his lord was, as it were, the rent he paid for his land.

In the twelfth century the custom began to be common for the lord, who was frequently for long periods absent on the Crusades or at war, to lease some of his land to tenants, instead of farming it all through bailiffs. This was found to be both easier and more profitable; and thus arose the farmer class. A still greater change was the gradual rise of the free labourer. The Church had long used its influence to urge men to give freedom to their serfs.

It was possible also for a serf to gain freedom by living a year and a day within the walls of a chartered town. The tenants, as they increased in wealth and social importance, found the labour-rent more and more burdensome. On the other hand, the lords, owing to the increasing luxury of the time and to the expenses of chivalry and war, were continually in want of money. It became, therefore, the custom for the serfs to buy their freedom from their lords. Edward III. himself used to raise money by selling manumissions to his serfs. In time the labourer became detached from the soil, and could pass from one farm to another.

The scarcity of labour after the Black Death made the landholders feel how disadvantageous this system was to them. Formerly they could compel their serfs to work. Now they had to pay the labourers the wages which they asked, or allow their land to remain untilled, and the harvests to rot upon the fields. Government was, of course, in those days entirely in the interests of the landlords. To remedy the evil of high wages, the king assembled his council on the 14th June, 1349. The country was not yet sufficiently recovered from the plague to allow of Parliament being summoned. The council issued a royal ordinance, which was afterwards embodied in the Statute of Labourers.

The preamble of this statute gives us in a few words a vivid picture of the times. It states that:

> A great part of the people, and especially of workmen and servants, late died of the pestilence. Many, seeing the necessity of masters and the great scarcity of servants, will not serve unless they may receive excessive wages; and some are rather willing to beg in idleness than by labour to get their living.

It then proceeds to ordain that all men and women who do not live by merchandise or by the exercise of any craft are to work for the same wages as they had received before the plague. They were to work first for their own lord, though he was not to retain more than he wanted. The statute went on to say that:

"seeing that many sturdy beggars, as long as they can live by begging and charity, refuse to labour, no one, under pain of imprisonment, shall presume to nourish them in their idleness." Thus the law ordered that all men were to work; giving alms to beggars was forbidden; the scale of wages was fixed, and men were once more bound, at least in the first place, to work for their lord.

The fixing of the scale of wages by law could have no permanent effect. With the high price of provisions, which had resulted from the Black Death, it was impossible for men to live on the same wages as before the plague. We see by the repeated reinforcements of the statute during the reign of Edward III. how unsuccessful it was in obtaining the desired result. Still more galling to the labourer was the attempt made by this statute to bind him once more to the soil, and thus to rob him of his newly-acquired freedom. We cannot wonder that the Statute of Labourers produced a growing discontent amongst the labour class, which at last broke out in the peasants' revolt under Richard II.

The horrors of the Black Death had rudely disturbed the joy and prosperity of the English people. No greater contrast can be imagined than that between the condition of England in 1347, when the people revelled in the enjoyment of peace and of a luxury unknown before, and England in the beginning of 1350. More than half the people had died of the plague; even amongst the cattle the mortality had been very great. The looms stood silent for want of weavers; the harvests lay rotting on the fields for want of labourers; sheep and oxen wandered half wild over the country because there was no one to tend them. The country pulpits remained silent. The people as well as their sheep were without shepherds. All suits and pleadings in the King's Bench, and all sessions of Parliament, ceased for two years. War was impossible. France was decimated by the plague as much as England, and a truce for two years was concluded between the two countries.

The population soon recovered its losses. The nobles had suffered comparatively little by the plague, and soon returned to their luxurious amusements. Preachers and moralists might declaim against the extravagances of fashion and dress, and say that the plague had been sent as a scourge from God, but the nobles clung to their fashions all the same. It was the people who had suffered by the plague, and felt its effects. Wheat was scarce, the price of provisions was exorbitantly high, and yet the law was striving to diminish wages. The life of the agricultural labourer in those days was at best very wretched. The articles of diet were few. The people lived on salt meat half the year. They had neither potatoes, carrots, nor parsnips; their only vegetables were onions, cabbages, and nettles. Spices were quite out of the reach of the common people. Sugar was a costly luxury. We can hardly realize the dreariness of the long winter nights in the dark and ill-ventilated huts, from which the smoke escaped as best it could. The people must have spent much of their time in darkness, as candles were too dear for them to buy.

But wretched as his surroundings might be, the labourer was not without intelligence. It was his ambition to send one of his sons to the university, that he might become a priest. So general was this custom that Parliament petitioned Edward III. to prohibit it, because the landlords feared that thus they might lose useful labourers. The distress of the peasantry under the Statute of Labourers, and the tyranny and oppression of their landlords, soon led them to form combinations among themselves for the defence of their own rights. These combinations were maintained by subscriptions of money. We learn that the labourers gathered themselves together in "great routs, and agreed by such confederacy to resist their lords." These combinations paved the way for the revolt under Richard II. The agricultural labourers throughout the country could communicate with one another by means of preachers who wandered over the country, and who, being men of the people themselves, shared the interests of their class.

In attempting to form any true idea of the condition of the lower orders of society in those times, of their hardships and grievances, we are much aided by the poem of William Langland, called the *Vision of Piers the Plowman*. Langland himself was an obscure man, of whom little certain is known. He seems to have been born about 1332, and to have been a secular priest. Three versions of his poem exist, the first written in 1362, the last about 1380. It is a long poem written in the old alliterative metre, that is, the rhyme is at the beginning, not at the end of the words. From a literary point of view the poem possesses little charm; its great interest lies in the light it throws on the social condition of the times.

Langland is an austere reformer. He is not like Chaucer, who likes to look on the bright side of things, and to take a genial view even of men's failings and sins, and make fun of them. He wishes to make men better by showing them their sin in its darkest colours, and pointing out the contrast between it and the virtue they ought to attain to. The poem is one long testimony against the sins of the rich, against the sins of all who do not *work*. If Chaucer has any distinct wish at all to make men better, he only tries to do it by making their sins ludicrous. In Langland's poem we never lose sight of the moral; the poet has no other purpose in writing than moral teaching. What he wishes to teach is simply this, that all men must work, though the work must differ in kind according to the rank of the worker. The knight's duty is to guard the Church from "wasters," and help the farmer by killing the hares, foxes, and wild birds. The ladies are to sew chasubles, to spin wool and flax, to clothe the naked, and to help all those who work worthily. If men will not work otherwise, hunger must make them do so. There are to be no beggars; even hermits must seize their spades and dig.

The dinner provided for the labourers after they have worked, shows us what the peasants had to live on in those days. Piers says he had no geese nor pigs, only cheese, curds, cream, oatcake, and loaves of beans and bran; and for vegetables, parsley, leeks, and cabbages. Besides these the poor people bought peascods, beans, apples and cherries, to feed hunger with. These were the things on which they must subsist till harvest time; then they would have better food, and good ale too.

Langland tells us that the people were beginning to be discontented with this kind of food. The beggars would eat only the finest bread; the labourers grew dainty, and were not content even with penny ale and a piece of bacon, but wanted fresh flesh and fried fish, and grumbled about their low wages.

Langland is very bitter against the indulgences granted by the priests for men's sins. A man can only obtain pardon by good works. The merchants must trade fairly, must repair hospitals and broken bridges, must dower maidens and aid poor scholars. He is more severe upon the lawyers than upon almost any other class; they take bribes, and will never speak unless you give them money first; only those who plead the cause of the poor, and do not need to be bought, can be saved. With crushing severity he dwells continually upon the sins of the clergy, and, like Wiclif, wishes for the return of the apostolical purity of the Church. The pestilence, he says, came simply as a punishment for men's sins. The whole poem is full of allusions to the questions of the day, and the severity of its criticisms is relieved by no playfulness, hardly by a single touch of humour.

In the form of his poem, Langland has followed the fashionable poets of his day, and has adopted the machinery of a dream. All that he tells us passed before him in a vision. Some few touches show that he too was not wanting in some growing sense of the beauties of nature, particularly in the opening of the poem, when he tells us that he wandered on the Malvern Hills on a May morning. When weary of wandering, he laid himself down

Under a broad bank, by a burn's side;
And as I lay, and leaned, and looked in the waters,
I slumbered in a sleeping, it sounded so merrily.

It is only the form, however, that Langland has taken from the fashionable poets of his day; of their spirit he has nothing. The beautiful side of chivalry was quite lost to him. He saw only its dark side, the luxury and selfish idleness to which it had led. He is a voice from the people, and as such is doubly interesting to us, since most of the chroniclers and writers of those times entirely disregarded the people, and spoke only of the upper ranks of society.

CHAPTER 7

Renewal of War with France

In 1350 the English were again troubled by rumours of war. The seamen of the Spanish ports on the Bay of Biscay had always been animated by hostility to the English, in whom they found formidable opponents to their commercial enterprises. They were full of zeal for mercantile adventure, and side by side with their commerce they committed many acts of piracy. They now assembled a large fleet, primarily with the object of trading with Flanders; but on their way to the Flemish ports they behaved more like pirates than merchants, and by claiming the dominion of the seas seemed to challenge the English to attack them.

At the Flemish ports the Spaniards loaded their ships with all kinds of rich merchandise, and prepared to return home, having no fear of the English; for the fleet was strong, and their admiral, De la Cerda, by promising liberal pay, had succeeded in enlisting a large number of volunteers at Sluys.

Froissart tells us that the King of England hated these Spaniards greatly, and said publicly:

> We have for a long time spared these people, for which they have done us much harm, without amending their conduct. On the contrary, they grow more arrogant; for which reason they must be chastised as they pass our coasts.

His son and his lords were only too ready to engage upon a warlike expedition. Edward summoned all gentlemen who at that time might be in England to meet him at Sandwich. Hither the queen too came to see them off.

The English fleet consisted of fifty sail; but the ships were far inferior to those of the Spaniards. Edward III. and the Black Prince each commanded a ship in person. For three days they cruised between Dover and Calais waiting the coming of the Spaniards. On the third day, when they hoped to engage, the king sat in the fore part of his ship, dressed in a black velvet jacket, and wearing on his head a small hat of beaver, which became him much. He was in most joyous spirits, and ordered his minstrels to play before him a German dance which Sir John Chandos had lately introduced. For his amusement he made Chandos sing with his minstrels, which delighted him greatly. From time to time he would ask his watch whether the Spaniards were in sight. At last, whilst the king was thus amusing himself with his knights, the watch cried out, "I spy a ship; and it appears to me to be a Spaniard."

At once the minstrels were silenced, and the king asked whether there was more than one ship. Soon the answer was shouted out, "Yes, I see two, three, four, and so many that, God help me, I cannot count them." Then the king and his knights knew that it was the Spanish fleet.

The trumpets sounded, and the ships were ordered to form in line of battle. It was already late; but the king was determined to engage. He called for wine, which he and his knights drank, and then stood ready to fight. The Spaniards might easily have avoided the battle, but hoping to crush their enemies, they sailed down upon them. Then Edward said to the captain of his ship, "Lay me alongside the Spaniard who is bearing down on us, for I will have a tilt with him." The shock of the meeting of the two ships was like the crash of a tempest.

The king's ship stood firm; but the Spaniard was much disabled, and lost her masts, so that the English knights cried to the king, "Let her go away; you shall have better than that." Then another large ship bore down, and grappled with chains and irons to that of the king, and the fight began in earnest. Many gallant deeds were done; but the Spanish ship proved hard to conquer. The king's ship was leaking, and in danger of sinking, only just in time was the Spanish ship boarded. The English threw all the men they found on it overboard; and leaving their own ship, continued the fight on board the Spaniard.

Meanwhile, the Prince of Wales was in great difficulty. His ship was grappled by an immense Spaniard, and was so full of holes that it was in great danger of sinking. The crew were employed in baling out water, and could not make head against the Spaniards. But the Duke of Lancaster, the prince's cousin, formerly Earl of Derby, seeing the danger, drew near, and fell on the other side of the enemy, grappling his ship to the Spaniard, with shouts of "Derby to the rescue." The ship was soon taken, and the crew were thrown overboard. The prince and his men, deserting their own ship, embarked on board the Spaniard.

It was a hard battle for the English, as the Spanish ships were very big and strong, and the Spaniards fought with extreme bravery, and knew no fear. At last victory declared itself for the English. The Spaniards lost fourteen ships, and the others saved themselves by flight. When it was over Edward sounded his trumpets for retreat, and the fleet sailed back to the English coast, anchoring off Rye and Winchelsea. The king and the prince landed, and the same night rode to the house where the queen was—just two leagues distant. She was most joyful at seeing them return safely, for she had been in great anxiety all day. Her servants had watched the battle from the hills on the coast, whence they could see it well, as the weather was fine and clear, and they had seen the great strength of their enemy, and their fine large ships. So great were the rejoicings that, instead of resting after the battle, the king and his knights spent the night in revelry with the ladies, talking of arms and love. The next morning the king thanked his knights for their services, and dismissed them.

This battle was the beginning of the rivalry between the English and the Spaniards for the dominion of the seas. The hardy Spanish seamen were not in the least depressed by their defeat. Both sides, however, soon saw that the quarrel was to the interests of neither, and a truce for twenty years was concluded in London between the King of England and the maritime cities of Castile. It must be remembered that the quarrel was not at all between the King of Castile and the King of England, but only between these maritime cities and the English naval power.

Attempts had been again made at a conference at Guisnes between the envoys of France and England to change the armistice between the two countries into a permanent peace. Edward III. offered to give up his claim to the French crown, if the French king would give up his claim of homage for the English provinces in France. When the French king refused to do this, Edward determined to begin the war again.

Philip of Valois, King of France, had died in 1350, and was succeeded by his son John. John found the treasury of France already impoverished by the expenses of the war, and did not make matters better by his unwise and prodigal liberality. His easy-going temper earned for him the name of the Good, though he brought his kingdom to the very verge of ruin. He wanted money for his favourites and his pleasures, and when he had taxed the people till they could give no more, he tried to get money by debasing the coinage, that is, he caused money containing a large quantity of alloy to be made, and obliged the people to take this bad money in exchange for their good money. This and his heavy taxes brought great misery and poverty upon the people, who were still suffering from the effects of the Black Death.

The country also suffered greatly from the Free Companies who roamed about in all directions, committing robberies and every kind of crime. These Free Companies were the plague of the Middle Ages. They were bands of mercenary soldiers ready to fight for anyone who would pay them, and when in intervals of peace they were dismissed from service they spent the time in plunder, in defiance of all laws and government. Froissart tells us that, in the year 1351, there was the greatest scarcity of provisions ever known in the memory of man, all over the kingdom of France. But in spite of the sufferings of his people, King John was eager for war and anxious to wash out the stain left on the French arms by the battle of Cressy. Edward was equally ready; even during the years when negotiations for peace had been going on, the truce had not really been observed, and both French and English had made many aggressions upon the enemy's country.

When in 1354 the Congress at Guisnes broke up, having accomplished nothing, Edward began to hasten his preparations for a new invasion of France. He had gained a new and important ally against John in the person of Charles, King of Navarre. This man was the evil genius of France during the years that followed. His crimes and unscrupulous ambition gained for him the surname of the Bad. He was one of the most powerful vassals of France, as he had inherited the earldom of Normandy and Evreux. To secure his friendship, King John had given him his daughter in marriage. But Charles soon incurred the hatred of John by murdering the king's favourite and chief counsellor. He had to fly from court, and in his absence John invaded Normandy and took some of his fortresses.

Charles determined to revenge this injury by aiding Edward III. against the King of France. He promised to give the English king possession of several strong fortresses in Normandy, so that he might land his troops there, and be able to advance to Paris in safety. At the same time Edward received a visit from some of the Gascon nobles, who came to ask him to send his son to lead them against the French. A great invasion of France by three separate armies was therefore planned. One, under the Black Prince, was to land at Bordeaux; a second, under the Duke of Lancaster, was to go and aid the Countess de Montfort in Britany; and a third, under Edward himself, was to invade Normandy.

Edward III. took a proud army with him to France; but he did not do much. His ally, Charles of Navarre, made peace with John, so that Edward was obliged to change his plans and land at Calais instead of Cherbourg. John was wise enough to give Edward no chance of a battle, whilst he urged upon the Scots to invade England in the absence of its king. News was brought to Edward in France that the Scots had crossed the border and retaken Berwick. He was obliged to return to resist them, and punished their inroad by invading Scotland, and spreading such destruction wherever he went, that the Scots long spoke of the time of this invasion as "Burnt Candlemas."

CHAPTER 8

Poitiers

The Black Prince had sailed from Plymouth on September 8th, 1355, with a large band of nobles. He was received at Bordeaux with great joy by all the nobles of the country. The Gascon lords were eager to fight under the banner of so brave a prince, and to distinguish themselves by feats of arms. They had long been annoyed by the inroads of the French, and they now begged the prince to lead them on a foraging expedition into France. They formed no plan for a campaign. The expedition was simply undertaken from love of plunder, and of fighting for its own sake. The prince had the absolute command, and had been appointed the king's lieutenant in Aquitaine. The expedition which he now undertook shows us the dark side of chivalry. We see him and his young knights, in wanton love of adventure, spreading ruin and destruction over the fairest provinces of France.

On leaving Bordeaux he divided his army into several "battles." These were to march at some distance from one another, that they might devastate a larger extent of country. In this way they went through Armagnac to the foot of the Pyrenees. Then the prince turned northwards to Toulouse, where he waited, hoping in vain that the French might be provoked to battle. He next crossed the Garonne, and went to Carcassone, a rich and populous city, as large as York. The inhabitants fled in terror, leaving the city gates open. The town was plundered and burnt, but the citadel stood firm, and the prince passed on without troubling to take it.

To save themselves from a like fate, the inhabitants of Montpelier destroyed their own suburbs, and the members of the ancient university fled to Avignon, to seek shelter with the Pope. Narbonne was one of the richest towns in France, and almost as large as London; it also was burnt and plundered. In eight weeks the Black Prince succeeded in ruining the richest district of France, from which the kings of France drew the chief part of their revenue. Peace had reigned there for more than a century, so that the inhabitants were ignorant of war and its horrors. Now five hundred towns and villages were smoking in ruins; the harvests were destroyed; everywhere there was devastation and ruin. The name of the Black Prince had become a terror, not only to the people whose peaceful homes he had destroyed, but to the whole of France.

Laden with booty, he and his knights returned to Bordeaux. Here the Gascon soldiers were dismissed till the spring, when an expedition into Poitou was talked of. The winter was spent by the Black Prince with his knights in great joy and festivity. There, the herald Chandos tells us, was "beauty and nobleness, sincerity, bounty and liberality." But neither were they quite idle; for in the course of the winter they succeeded in retaking such fortresses in Gascony as had been taken by the French.

It was not till the middle of the following summer that the Black Prince gathered his men together to start on a second campaign. He left Bordeaux on the 8th July with only a small force—2,000 men-at-arms and 6,000 archers—partly Gascons and partly English. His object was to make another foraging expedition, and, if possible, proceed onwards to join his cousin the Duke of Lancaster in Normandy. He went through Auvergne northward as far as Berry. Froissart tells us that they found the province of Auvergne very rich, and all things in great abundance. They burnt and destroyed all the country they passed through, and when they entered any town which was well provisioned, they rested there some days to refresh themselves, and on leaving destroyed what remained, staving the heads of wine casks and burning the wheat and oats, so that their enemies should not save anything. Everywhere they found plenty as they advanced, for the country was very rich and full of forage for men-at-arms.

At Vierzon, a town in Berry, they learnt that the King of France was at Chartres with a large army, and that all the passes and towns on the Loire were secured and so well guarded that no one could cross the river. The prince then held a council with his knights, and they resolved to return to Bordeaux through Touraine and Poitou, destroying all the country on their way. Near Romorantin some of the prince's men had a skirmish with some French soldiers, whom they routed. The castle of Romorantin refused to yield to the prince. As he was assailing it one of his squires was killed at his side by a stone thrown from the castle. The prince was so furious that he swore he would not leave that place till he had the castle and all in it in his power. Cannons were brought forward, and Greek-fire was shot upon the town, till a large Tower of the castle, covered with thatch, caught fire and was all in a blaze. Then the garrison had to yield; but the prince treated them nobly, and set many knights and squires at liberty, whilst he made the lords, who had commanded the castle, ride by his side and attend him as his prisoners.

When the King of France heard that the prince was hastening back to Bordeaux, he determined to pursue him, thinking that he could not escape. He left Chartres, and marched south, to intercept him on his way back. John was marching almost in a direct line south, whilst the Black Prince was marching from Romorantin in a south-westerly direction. It was therefore impossible but that they should meet. The English, however, were ignorant of their danger, till they accidentally discovered, when near Charigny, on September 17, by coming upon a French reconnoitring party, that the great French army was between them and Bordeaux. Escape was impossible. The Prince had only 8,000 men, while John had a mighty army of 50,000. But Prince Edward would rather fight even against such odds than yield to an enemy. All that remained for him was to choose his position well and fight his best. The skilful tactics displayed by the prince in disposing of his small force, show us that he was something more than merely a brave soldier.

King John sent Sir Eustace de Ribeaumont to reconnoitre the English. He brought back an account of the way in which they were posted, which has been preserved to us.

There were 2,000 men-at-arms, 6,000 archers, and about 1,000 camp followers quartered on a small hill which did not contain 2,000 square feet of ground. This hill was surrounded by very thick hedges, and was divided in the middle by a road, a little crooked and so narrow that hardly three men could go up it abreast. The road was covered on both sides with high hedges, behind which were encamped the archers, who were still at work making a new ditch. At the end of these hedges were the men-at-arms on foot, each holding his horse by his bridle; they were standing amidst vines and thorns, where it was impossible to march in any regular order. Before them were drawn up the archers, arranged in the manner of a harrow. On the left, where the hedges and the avenue were not so thick, the waggons were piled one upon another to make a barrier. Some cavalry were collected on

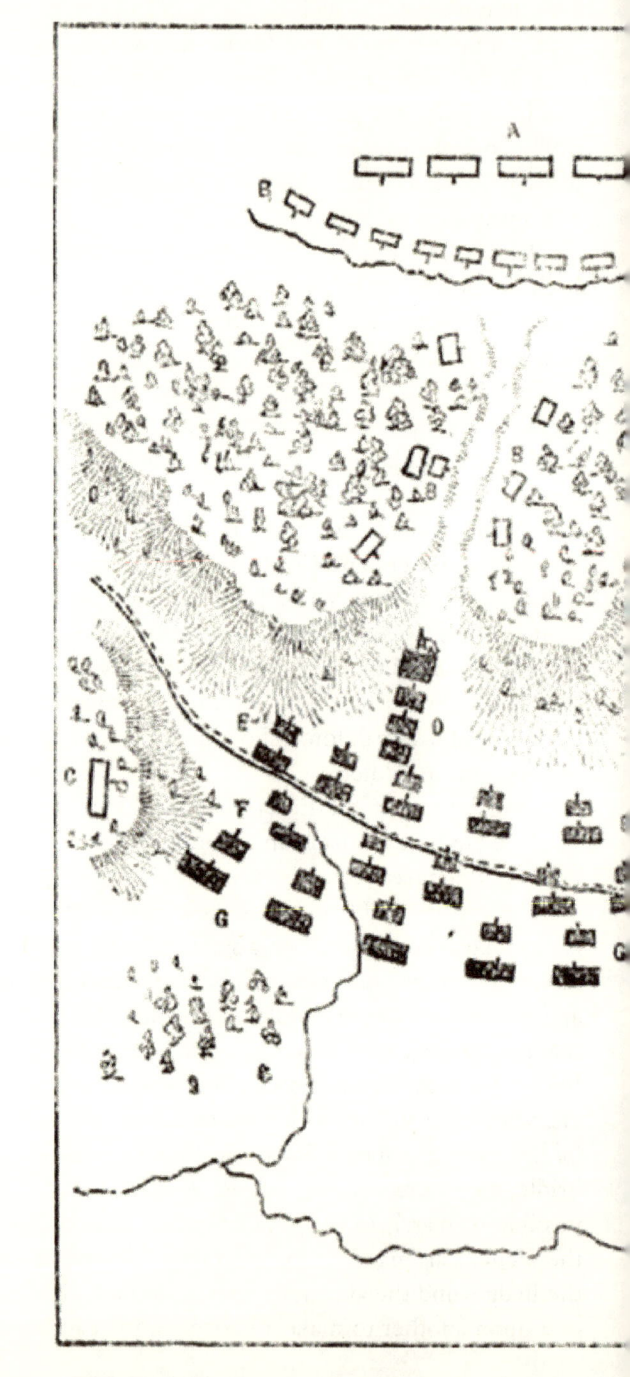

Plan of the
BATTLE of POITIERS,
19th September 1356.

▭	English
▬	French
A	Prince of Wales
B	Archers
C	Reserve
D	Marschalls (French)
E	Duke of Orleans
F	Dauphin
G	King John

Beauvoir

a little eminence to the right, that they might attack the enemy on the flanks.

On Sunday morning, September 18, King John was ready and impatient for the attack. He ordered a solemn mass to be sung in his tent, and he and his four sons partook of the communion. After some debate with his chief nobles, it was ordered that the whole army should push into the plain, and that each lord should display his banner, and advance in the name of God and St. Denis. The trumpets sounded, and every one mounted his horse, and made for that part of the plain where the king's banner was planted and fluttering in the wind. Froissart says:

> There might be seen all the nobility of France, richly dressed in brilliant armour, with banners and pennons gallantly displayed; for all the flower of the French nobility was there: no knight nor squire, for fear of dishonour, dared to remain at home.

And all this mighty force was going to attack a small body of 8,000 men, mostly simple archers, men of the people, standing at bay amidst the hedges and vineyards on the little hill.

When the French were on the point of marching against their enemies, the Cardinal of Perigord, who had left Poitiers that morning early, came at full gallop to the king, and making a deep reverence, begged him for the love of God to stay a minute. He said, with uplifted hands:

> Most dear sire, you have here all the flower of knighthood of your kingdom against a handful of people such as the English are. You may have them upon other terms than by a battle. I beseech you by the love of God let me go to the prince and remonstrate with him on the dangerous situation he is in."

Then the king answered, "It is agreeable to us, but make haste back again." The cardinal found the prince on foot in the thickest part of the vineyard, and when he asked him for permission to make up matters between him and the King of France, the prince replied, "Sir, my own honour and that of my army saved, I am ready to listen to reasonable terms." The cardinal then returned to John, and after much eloquent pleading succeeded in persuading him to consent to a truce till the next day at sunrise. The king ordered a very handsome and rich pavilion of red silk to be pitched on the spot where he stood, and dismissed his army to their quarters for the present.

All Sunday the cardinal rode from one army to another, and did his utmost to bring about a peaceful agreement. But the King of France would listen to nothing unless the Prince of Wales and one hundred of his knights surrendered themselves prisoners. To these terms the prince could not be expected to consent. On Monday morning the French almost angrily bade the cardinal begone and trouble them no more with his entreaties. Then he went to the Prince of Wales, and said, "Fair son, exert yourself as much as possible, for there must be a battle." The prince replied that such were his intentions, and those of his army, "and God defend the right." On the whole the cardinal did not meet with much gratitude from either side for his endeavours, and he went sadly back to Poitiers.

Sunday had been spent by the prince's men in making many mounds and ditches round the ground where the archers stood, to secure their position. They were much straitened for want of provisions, as they could not without danger move from their place to seek them. The French, on the other hand, were well supplied, and spent the day in the midst of plenty. When the prince saw on Monday morning that the battle was inevitable, and knew with what contempt the French regarded him and his men, he spoke thus to his army:

> Now, my gallant fellows, what though we be a small body when compared to the army of our enemies, do not let us be cast down on that account, for victory does not always follow numbers, but where the Almighty God pleases to bestow it. If through good fortune the day shall be ours, we shall gain the greatest honour and glory in this world; if the contrary should happen, and we be slain, I have a father and beloved brethren alive, and you all have some relations or good friends, who will be sure to revenge our deaths. I therefore beg you exert yourselves and fight manfully, for if it please God and St. George you shall see me this day act like a true knight.

With these and other words the prince and his marshals encouraged the men, so that they were all in high spirits.

Then the prince retired a little way apart, and kneeling down, prayed:

> Father Almighty, as I have ever believed that Thou art king over all kings, and that for us upon the cross Thou wert content to suffer death to save us from the pains of hell; Father, who art very God and very man, be pleased for Thy holy name to guard

me and my people from ill, even as, O heavenly Father, Thou knowest that I have good cause.

Then he was ready to fight. Sir John Chandos placed himself near the Prince to guard and advise him, and never during that day would he on any account quit his post.

As the battle was about to begin, Sir James Audley came to the prince, and told him that he had made a vow, that if ever he should be engaged in any battle where the king or any of his sons were, he would be foremost in the attack, and the best combatant on their side, or die in the attempt. Now he begged permission to leave the prince's side, and perform his vow. The prince consented; and holding out his hand to him, said, "Sir James, God grant that this day you may shine in valour above all other knights." Sir James then proceeded to the front, attended only by four squires. He was a prudent and a valiant knight, and the order in which the army had been arranged was owing in great part to his advice.

The French now began to advance. Before reaching the battalion of the prince they must pass up the narrow lane, where scarce three men could walk abreast, the sides of which were lined with rows of archers. It was certain death for those who advanced first; but the French knights were brave, and did not fear death. Two French marshals commanding a body of cavalry fearlessly entered the lane; but as soon as they were well enclosed, the archers let loose their flight of arrows. A deadly and persistent shower came from each side of the lane. The French horses, smarting under the pain of the wounds made by the arrows, would not advance, but turned about, and were so unruly as to throw their masters, who could not manage them.

So great was the confusion, that those who had fallen could not get up again. Trampled upon by the terrified horses and wounded by the arrows, they lay writhing on the ground in agony. Some few knights were so well mounted that, by the strength of their horses, they passed through and broke the hedge, but still could not succeed in getting up to the battalion of the prince. Sir James Audley stood in front of it with his four squires, performing prodigies of valour, and stayed not to make any prisoners.

The first battalion of the French was completely routed; for the English men-at-arms rushed in upon them as they were struck down by the archers, and seized and slew them at their pleasure. As this French battalion fell back, it prevented the main body of the army from advancing. The next battalion was commanded by the Duke of Normandy, King John's eldest son. It was seized by wild terror at seeing the retreat of the first battalion, and many knights mounted their horses and started off in flight. A body of English came down from the hill, and attacking their flank, completed their terror. The English archers shot so quickly and well that the French did not know which way to turn themselves to avoid their arrows.

Little by little the English men-at-arms advanced under cover of the shower of arrows sent by their archers. When they saw the first French battalion beaten, and the second in disorder, they mounted their horses, which they held by their bridles, and raised a shout of "St. George for Guienne." Sir John Chandos said to the prince:

> Sir, now push forward; for the day is ours. God will this day put it in your hand. Let us make for the King of France. Where he is will lie the main stress of the business. His valour will not let him fly. He will be ours, if it please God and St. George; but he must be well fought with. You have before said that you will show yourself this day a good knight.

The prince answered, "John, get forward; you shall not see me turn my back this day; for I will always be among the foremost."

As they advanced the battle grew very hot, and was greatly crowded. Many a one was unhorsed. The battalion of the Duke of Normandy, on seeing the prince's approach, hastened their flight. The king's three sons, who commanded it, were advised to fly, and galloped away. Many others followed their example, though there were not wanting some brave knights who preferred death to flight. Then the king's battalion advanced in good order. The king and his knights had dismounted. They despaired of the day, but were determined at least to save their honour. Fighting on foot, it was hard to resist the shock of the English men-at-arms; but the king fought with desperate bravery, and by his side fought his little son Philip, a boy of fifteen, who warned his father against unexpected blows. The bravery of the boy on that day earned for him the surname of *le hardi*, the bold. He is that Philip le Hardi afterwards so well known as Duke of Burgundy.

King John proved himself a good knight; if the fourth of his people had behaved as well, the day would have been his own. Round him his knights too fought with great courage. Many were slain at his side, and others were obliged to yield themselves prisoners. The king himself was twice wounded in the face, but still fought bravely on. Many of the English who knew him pressed round in eagerness to take him, crying out, "Surrender yourself, or you are a dead man."

He was getting very roughly treated, when a young knight, called Denys Morbeque, forced his way through the medley, and bade the king surrender to him.

Then the king turned to him, and said, "To whom shall I surrender myself? Where is my cousin, the Prince of Wales? If I could see him I would speak to him."

"Sire," answered Denys, "he is not here; but surrender yourself to me, and I will lead you to him."

Then the king asked who he was; and on learning, gave him his right hand glove, and said, "I surrender myself to you."

Meanwhile the Prince of Wales had been fighting with the courage of a lion. Sir John Chandos, who had never left his side, now said to him, "Sir, it will be right for you to halt here, and plant your banner on the top of this bush, that you may rally your scattered forces. I do not see any banners or pennons of the French. They cannot rally again, and you must refresh yourself a little, as you are very much heated." Then the banner of the Prince was placed on a high bush. The minstrels began to play, and the trumpets and clarions to sound. The prince took off his helmet to cool himself, and his attendants soon pitched a small pavilion of crimson cloth, into which he entered. Wine was given him and his knights to drink. Every minute fresh knights kept arriving. They were returning from the pursuit, which was carried even to the gates of Poitiers, and now stopped with their prisoners at the prince's tent.

The prince asked eagerly for news of the King of France. None had seen him leave his battalion; he must be either killed or a prisoner. Immediately the prince ordered two of his barons, the Earl of Warwick and Lord Cobham, to ride off and learn what they could about the king. They soon came upon a crowd of men-at-arms, English and Gascon, who had snatched the King of France from the knight who had first taken him, and were now disputing who should have him. The king, feeling himself in danger, entreated them to take him and his son in a courteous manner to the prince, as he was great enough to make them all rich. The two barons forced their way through the crowd, and ordered them, under pain of instant death, to retreat. Then dismounting they greeted the king with profound reverence, and led him quietly to the prince's tent. The prince on seeing his royal prisoner made him a low bow, and gave him such comfort as he could.

He ordered wine and spices to be brought, and himself waited on the king.

The battle had begun at nine in the morning, and was over at noon. But not till dusk did the English return from the pursuit of their enemies. So great was the number of prisoners, that the English feared that it might be difficult to keep them all, and thought it wiser to ransom a great part of them on the spot. Such was the confidence inspired by chivalry in a man's word, that many were released on their promise of coming to Bordeaux before Christmas to pay their ransom. No fewer than seventeen counts were among the prisoners, and six thousand men lay dead upon the field. The English encamped that night on the battle-field amidst the dead. Many of them had hardly tasted bread for three days. Now they had abundance of all things, for the French had brought great stores of provisions with them. Besides provisions, they gained also quantities of gold and silver plate, rich jewels, and furred mantles. The French Army had come, confident of victory, provided with magnificent dresses and luxuries of all kinds.

That evening the Prince of Wales gave a supper in his pavilion to the King of France. The food served had all been taken from the French, as the English had nothing. The French king, with his son and his principal barons, was seated at the chief table, and was waited upon by the prince himself, who showed every mark of humility. He would not sit down at the table, though pressed to do so, but said that he was not worthy of so great an honour; nor did it become him to seat himself at the table of so great a king, or of so valiant a man as he had shown himself by his actions that day. He did his utmost to cheer the king, saying:

> Dear sir, do not make a poor meal because the Almighty God has not gratified your wishes in the event of this day. Be assured that my father will show you every honour and friendship in his power, and will arrange your ransom so reasonably that you will henceforward always remain friends. In my opinion, you have cause to be glad that the success of this battle did not turn out as you desired; for you have this day acquired such high renown for prowess, that you have surpassed all the best knights on your side. I do not say this, dear sir, to flatter you; for all on our side who saw the deeds of both parties agree that this is your due, and award you the prize and garland for it."

This little speech was greeted with murmurs of applause from every one. The French said the prince had spoken nobly and truly, and that he would be one of the most gallant princes in Christendom, if God should grant him life to pursue his career of glory.

After supper the English repaired to their several tents, each taking with him the knights or squires he had captured. They soon came to agreement about ransoms, as the English lords were not greedy in their demands, and asked no more than each man declared he could pay. The next morning they rose early and heard mass. After breakfast, whilst the servants packed up the baggage, their lords decamped, and the army began its march to Bordeaux.

The Minorites of the convent of Poitiers took upon themselves the melancholy task of burying the dead. The bodies were carried in carts, and buried in large graves in their churchyard. Funeral masses were sung in all the churches and convents of the town of Poitiers, at the cost of the good citizens of the town.

So was fought the great battle of Poitiers, a signal instance of what a small force can do when skilfully posted and fighting for its life. The French Army failed through their excess of confidence in their proud strength. The first rebuff was so unexpected that it struck terror into the whole army, and made them fly before a quarter of their number had been really engaged in battle. Of the English, few fought more bravely than Sir James Audley, who was badly wounded. The prince inquired for him after the battle, and caused him to be carried in a litter to the spot where he was standing. Then he bent down over him and embraced him, saying that he had acquired glory and renown above them all, and proved himself the bravest knight. As a reward, he endowed him with a yearly income of five hundred *marks*. This pension Sir James afterwards divided between the four squires who had fought so bravely with him; and when the prince learnt this, he praised him much for his generosity.

Bravest, and at the same time most modest, of all the knights was the prince himself. Two letters are still preserved in which he gives an account of the battle, one to the Bishop of Worcester, and one to the city of London. In each he tells the simplest story of his victory, taking no credit to himself. In his letter to the city of London, after describing the events which led up to the battle of Poitiers, he says, "For default of victuals, as well as for other reasons, it was agreed that we should take our way, flanking them in such manner, that if they wished for battle, or to draw towards us in a place that was not very much to our disadvantage, we should be the first; and so forthwith it was done. Whereupon battle was joined on the eve of the day before St. Matthew (21st September), and, God be praised for it, the enemy was discomfited, and the king was taken and his son, and a great number of other great people were both slain and taken, as our chamberlain, the bearer hereof, who has very full knowledge thereon, will know how more fully to inform and show you, as we are not able to write to you."

CHAPTER 9

Triumphal Return to England

On leaving the battlefield of Poitiers, the little army of English, with many prisoners and rich booty, did not venture to attack any fortress on their way to Bordeaux; it would be honour enough to take back in safety the King of France and his son, and all the gold and silver and jewels they had won. They proceeded by slow marches, as they were heavily laden. They met with no resistance. The whole country was subdued by terror, and the men-at-arms retreated into the fortresses.

When the prince drew near to Bordeaux, all the people came out to welcome him. First came the college of Bordeaux, in solemn procession, bearing crosses and chanting thanksgivings. They were followed by all the dames and damsels of the town, both old and young, with their attendants. The prince led the king to the monastery of St. Andrew, where they both lodged, the king on one side and the prince on the other. The citizens and the clergy made great feasts for the prince, and showed much joy at his victory. Soon after his arrival the Cardinal of Perigord came to Bordeaux as ambassador from the Pope, who sent a letter to the Black Prince, exhorting him to use his victory moderately, and to make peace. During the following winter the Black Prince stayed at Bordeaux, where he and his Gascon and English soldiers passed the time in feasting and merriment, and lavishly spent all the gold and silver they had gained. When the news of the battle of Poitiers was brought to England, by a messenger bearing King John's helmet and coat of mail, it was received with great rejoicings throughout the country. Thanksgivings were offered up in all the churches, and bonfires were made in every town and village.

As the spring drew near, the prince began to make preparations for taking his royal prisoners to England. When the season was sufficiently advanced, he called together the chief Gascon lords, and told them what preparations he had made, and how he was going to leave the country under their care. But the Gascons were not at all pleased on learning that he meant to take the King of France away with him to England. They looked upon John as their prisoner, and did not wish to lose him. When the prince could not pacify them, Sir John Chandos and Lord Cobham, who knew well how dearly the Gascons loved gold, advised him to offer them a handsome sum of money. After receiving a hundred thousand florins the Gascons consented that the King of France should depart. The Black Prince embarked in a fine ship, taking with him some Gascon lords. The King of France went in a ship by himself, so that he might be more at his ease.

Before making up his mind to return to England the Black Prince had concluded, on the 14th March, 1357, through the mediation of the Pope, a truce of two years with the regency, which was ruling France during the captivity of her king. He was thus able to leave Aquitaine without fear of its being attacked by the French during his absence. The voyage to England lasted eleven days and nights, and the little fleet reached Sandwich on May 4th, 1357. The prince, with his royal prisoners and his attendants, remained two days at Sandwich that they might refresh themselves after their voyage. Their next stopping-place was Canterbury, which in those days none would pass without turning aside to worship at the shrine of the famous martyr, St. Thomas of Canterbury, in the great cathedral. Here the King of France and the Black Prince knelt, and worshipped, and made their offerings. The second night they rested at Rochester; the third night at Dartford.

As soon as Edward III. had heard of their arrival in England, he gave orders for preparations to be made for their triumphal entry into London. All the great gilds of the city were ordered to appear in procession with the banners. The twelve great gilds, the Livery Companies of the city, the Merchant Taylors, Goldsmiths, Leathersellers, and the unions of the artificers of special crafts, were then at the very summit of their wealth and importance. They possessed exclusive privileges with regard to their special trade, which none might practise except members of the gild. Admission into the gild was almost impossible, as the aim of the gild brothers was to make their crafts monopolies of a few families. These gilds were possessed of enormous wealth, and ruled the city of London. So important were they, that Edward III. himself, as well as the Black Prince, became members of the gild of

Merchant Taylors. Now the gilds were ordered to prepare a grand reception for the Prince of Wales and his prisoners. Each gild went out, headed by its warden, with its banners borne before. Mounted on horseback, 1,000 of the chief citizens went out to Southwark to meet the prince.

The King of France rode a splendid white courser; the Black Prince was mounted on a little black hobby, and rode by the king's side. Escorted by this great body of citizens, they entered London. First they had to cross London Bridge, which was very different then from what it is now. It was a stone bridge of twenty arches, with a large drawbridge in the middle. On either side of the bridge was a row of high and stately houses; in the middle was a Gothic chapel, dedicated to St. Thomas of Canterbury. At either end was a fortified gateway with battlements and a portcullis, and on the battlements were stuck the ghastly heads of traitors. The procession passed over the bridge, watched by wondering crowds, and on through the narrow streets, with their quaint overhanging gabled houses, mostly built of wood.

It proceeded up Cornhill, where the corn merchants held their traffic, along Cheapside, past the Cathedral of St. Paul's, and then along Fleet Street. Everywhere the houses were decorated with tapestry hung outside the walls; and the rich citizens exposed at their windows their splendid plate, and quantities of armour, bows and arrows, and all kinds of arms. Through Temple Bar, the procession passed out into the Strand, which then ran through green fields to Westminster. Here and there, on either side of the road, were the houses of the nobles and the bishops, surrounded by gardens. They passed the Savoy Palace, one of the largest of these houses, which was to be the abode of King John during his captivity, and Whitehall, then the palace of the Archbishop of York. At last they came to Westminster.

So dense had been the crowd of spectators blocking the narrow streets that the cavalcade could only advance very slowly; and though they had entered the city at three o'clock in the morning, it was not till noon, nine hours afterwards, that they reached Westminster. Edward III. received them in Westminster Hall, seated on a throne, surrounded by his prelates and barons. He greeted John with every possible honour and distinction, descending from his throne to embrace him. He then led him to partake of a splendid banquet prepared in his honour. That afternoon the clergy of London came forth in procession, clad in their robes, and bearing crosses in their hands, and marched through the streets, singing psalms of praise. For two days prayers and thanksgivings were offered up throughout London and Westminster.

King John had an apartment in the king's own palace at Westminster till the Savoy Palace was prepared for him and his son. He was afterwards removed to Windsor, and then to Hertford Castle. The winter after his arrival splendid jousts were held in Smithfield. King John and his son, as well as the French lords who had been brought as prisoners to England, were allowed, on giving their parole, great liberty in England. They amused themselves principally in hunting and hawking in the forests around Windsor. The number of Frenchmen at that time in England led the English courtiers to imitate French fashions. Before the taking of King John the English used to wear beards, and their hair was cropped short round their heads. Now they copied the French, and wore their hair in flowing locks, and shaved their beards.

Edward III. and his queen paid frequent visits to the King of France, and often invited him to sumptuous entertainments, doing their utmost to cheer and console him. Edward was anxious to release John as soon as possible; but he asked such an enormous ransom, that it was hopeless to obtain it, in the impoverished condition of France.

The state of France was indeed deplorable. The regent, Prince Charles the *dauphin*, had summoned the States General to meet at Paris, to do something for the restoration of order and government. They proved very unmanageable, and complained of the misgovernment of the country, of the over taxation which had ruined the people, and of the wasteful prodigality which had emptied the exchequer. The leading spirit in the States General was Etienne Marcel, provost of the merchants of Paris. He hoped to be able to set on foot all kinds of reforms, and succeeded in releasing from prison Charles the Bad, King of Navarre.

Charles had managed to gain the sympathy of the people of Paris by his imprisonment, which they looked upon as unjust. He now promised to befriend the people's interests. He and Marcel harangued the populace of Paris, and increased their zeal for reforms. Meanwhile the people in the country were suffering the most horrible poverty. The barons, who had been taken prisoners at Poitiers, returned on parole in haste to their estates, to collect the money necessary for their ransom. To raise this money, all the small possessions of the peasants on their estates were seized and sold. Ruined by their lords, the peasants were next subject to the cruelties of the free companies, which were now more numerous than ever.

After the Battle of Poitiers, the disbanded French soldiers, the soldiers of the King of Navarre, many Gascons, and even many English, had formed themselves into companies. These were commanded, not by common soldiers or by low-born persons, but by barons and nobles; one was even commanded by the brother of the King of Navarre. In the absence of their king, the barons seem to have broken loose from all restraint, and ravaged the country at pleasure. These companies kept the whole land in terror. They *devested* the country, and sacked the cities; even Paris trembled at their approach. The country people hid themselves in caves in the earth to escape them.

At last, driven to despair by hunger and suffering, the peasants rose in fury. They attacked the castles, plundered and burnt them, and murdered the nobles with their wives and families. It was a terrible and desperate vengeance for the outrages and oppressions of many centuries. The nobles had long spoken contemptuously of the peasants as "*Jacques bonhomme*," and from this the rising of the peasants was called the Jacquerie. It was soon crushed. The nobles, forgetting all distinctions of party, turned as one man against the peasants. Charles of Navarre laid aside his character of a popular leader, and was foremost in massacring the revolted peasants. Marcel alone tried to send them aid, as indeed it was in his interest to support the people against the nobility.

The suppression of the revolt left the country in a more miserable condition than before. Marcel's position in Paris was becoming dangerous. He was besieged in the city by the army of the *dauphin*, and to save himself determined to give over the city into the hands of Charles of Navarre. In the very act of giving up the keys he was murdered by the partisans of the *dauphin*, and died after having done something for his country by the reforms which he had wrung from the *dauphin*. After his death the *dauphin* entered Paris, but was powerless until he consented to make peace with Charles of Navarre, for the whole country was overrun by English and Navarrese soldiers.

The *dauphin* was at Paris with his brothers. No merchants or others dared to venture out of the city to look after their concerns or take any journey, for they were attacked and killed whatever road they took. The Navarrese were masters of all the rivers, and most of the cities. This caused such a scarcity of provisions that we are told that a small cask of herrings sold for thirty golden crowns, and other things in proportion. Many died of hunger; salt was so dear that the inhabitants of the large towns were greatly distressed for want of it. By a reconciliation with the King of Navarre, the *dauphin* hoped to free the country from the ravages of the Navarrese soldiers, and to be able to offer some resistance to the English.

But however deplorable the condition of France might be, it could hardly be expected that it would accept peace on the conditions offered by the English. The truce which had existed between England and France since the Battle of Poitiers came to an end on the 1st May, 1359. The King of England and the Prince of Wales had a meeting with King John at Westminster, and John showed himself willing to sign any treaty that was proposed to him. The English demanded that all the country from Calais to the Pyrenees, even Normandy and Anjou, should be given up to them, and that four millions of golden florins should be paid as King John's ransom. When this treaty was brought to France, the *dauphin* assembled the King of Navarre and others in a council of state, and laid it before them.

It was unanimously rejected. "We would rather endure," they answered, "the great distress we are in at present than suffer the kingdom of France to be diminished. King John must remain longer in England." When Edward III. heard their answer, he said that before the winter was over he would enter France with a powerful army, and remain there until there was an end of the war by an honourable and satisfactory peace.

Chapter 10

The Peace of Bretigny

England all this time was in a condition of peaceful prosperity; the king and his court were amusing themselves with tournaments and hunting parties. Edward III. determined to open the war again, and began his preparations for leading a mighty army into France. Swarms of adventurers of all nations gathered at Calais, and offered him their services. The Duke of Lancaster was also to come to Calais, and bring with him the English troops which had been fighting for the cause of the De Montforts in Brittany.

On 28th October, 1359, Edward sailed from Sandwich with an army such as had not been raised in England for more than a hundred years. Froissart tells us that there was not a knight or a squire, from the age of twenty to sixty, who did not go. It is interesting to note, that amongst those who took part in this expedition was Geoffrey Chaucer, then only a young man, but destined to become famous as the first great name in our list of English poets. The king took with him the Black Prince, and three of his other sons, Lionel, John, and Edmund.

On landing at Calais, Edward proceeded to arrange his battalions, that he might set off at once to meet the Duke of Lancaster. First marched the king's battalion, and after it an immense baggage train, which Froissart tells us was two leagues in length. It consisted of more than five thousand carriages, drawn by horses, and carrying provisions for the army. They were well provided with all kinds of things which no English army had ever taken with it before, such as mills to grind their corn, and ovens to bake their bread. After the king's battalion came the battalion of the Prince of Wales, who was accompanied by his brothers. The men-at-arms were all so richly dressed, and rode such fine horses, that, says Froissart, it was a pleasure to look at them. Both they and the archers marched in close order, that they might be ready to engage at any moment, should it be necessary. With the army went five hundred pioneers, with spades and pickaxes to level the roads, and cut down trees and hedges, so that the carriages might pass easily. The Duke of Lancaster's battalion joined them soon after leaving Calais, and the three battalions proceeded on their march into the heart of France.

They did not advance very quickly, as they had to let all the waggons keep pace with them. They found no provisions on their way, as everything had been carried off to supply the garrisons. Moreover the country had been so pillaged and destroyed that the ground had not been cultivated for three years. They had hoped to refresh themselves in the vineyards, and lay in stores of the new wine; but the season was so rainy that the grapes were worth nothing. Day and night the rain fell in torrents; but, in spite of all difficulties, and though winter was coming on, they pressed on to Rheims, avoiding all the other strong towns; for it was Edward's ambition to be crowned at Rheims, in the cathedral where the kings of France were always crowned.

Rheims was a strong town, and was well defended by its archbishop. Edward wished to reduce it by a long siege, not to storm it, for he was careful of his men. The English Army therefore quartered itself in different villages round the town. The king, the Black Prince, and the Duke of Lancaster each kept their court in different places, and had great households. Many of the counts and barons were not so comfortable, as the rainy weather still continued, and their horses were badly housed and ill fed. There was a great scarcity of corn of all kinds. One of the English knights succeeded in taking a little town near Rheims, in which he found three thousand butts of wine, great part of which he sent to the King of England and his sons, to their great joy. The knights often wearied of the siege, and went away on little expeditions by themselves, and there were many brave passages of arms between them and the French.

For seven weeks Edward III. remained before Rheims, and then began to tire of the siege. It was hopeless to try and take the city by assault, for it was well defended. Many of the horses had perished, owing to the scarcity of fodder; so at last he determined to break up his camp. He marched south from Rheims to Chalons and Tonnerre. At Tonnerre, he found very good wines, and in order to enjoy them, stayed there five days. He then went on further south still, to Flavigny, where he spent the whole of Lent, because there was a good store of provisions there. His light troops scoured the country, and constantly brought in fresh provisions.

The men-at-arms amused themselves in many different ways. They had brought with them from England a number of boats, made, says Froissart, surprising well, of boiled leather; these would hold three men, who could then go fishing in little rivers and lakes. They were able to catch a great deal of fish, which was very useful, as during Lent, according to the rules of the Church, no meat might be eaten. The king had with him thirty falconers on horseback, with their hawks, sixty couple of strong hounds and as many greyhounds, and amused himself every day with hunting and hawking. Many of his lords also had their hawks and hounds.

Flavigny was in the Duke of Burgundy's dominions. He was a vassal of the King of France, but in reality ruled like an independent prince. He therefore sent ambassadors, and made a treaty with Edward, so that his country might not be destroyed. When the treaty was signed the English army broke up their camp, and went on towards Paris by forced marches.

Whilst Edward was in Burgundy, England had been alarmed by the appearance of a French fleet, which ravaged the English coast, and even took and pillaged Winchelsea. With great difficulty the English succeeded in raising a small fleet, before which the French retired, and the English revenged themselves for the French outrages by ravaging the coast of France. When news of this French invasion reached Edward, it must doubtless have made him more anxious than ever to force a peace from the French, so that he might not lose any of the advantages which he had already won. He established himself at a short distance from Paris, and sent heralds to the *dauphin*, who was in the city, offering him battle; but the *dauphin* would not venture outside the walls of Paris. This greatly enraged the king, and he allowed Sir Walter Manny and other knights to assault the barriers of Paris; but they could not do much, as the city was well defended. The army was exhausted by the sufferings endured on account of the rainy winter, and the scarcity of provisions. Edward determined, therefore, to take them along the Loire to Britany to recruit and refresh themselves; and then after the vintage, which promised to be a very good one, to bring them again to lay siege to Paris.

Meanwhile, Pope Innocent VI. had been doing his utmost to persuade the *dauphin* to make peace, who at last consented to send commissioners after the King of England to try and arrange terms. It was hard to persuade Edward to give up his ambition to be king of France;

but at last he listened to the arguments of his cousin, the Duke of Lancaster, whom he much loved and trusted, and who showed him how doubtful it was that he could hope to succeed in his ambitious desires, whilst the war might easily last out his lifetime.

Froissart tells us that a sudden storm of hail and thunder so frightened the English Army, that they thought the world was come to an end. Edward, looking upon it as a judgment from God, vowed to the Virgin to accept terms of peace.

At last, at the little village of Bretigny, near Chartres, a treaty was signed on May 8th, 1360. This peace, known as the peace of Bretigny, is most important in history; it serves as a sort of landmark in the midst of the wars and struggles of the middle ages. In this treaty Edward promised to give up forever his claim to the throne of France, and to all the dominions of the Angevine kings north of the Loire—Anjou, Maine, Tourraine, and Normandy; he retained only Calais. On the other hand, the kings of France were to give up forever all right of exacting homage for the English provinces of Guienne and Gascony. Britany was not included in the treaty, and England and France were both at liberty to assist either of the competitors for the duchy. King John was to be ransomed for 3,000,000 golden crowns, equal to about £30,000,000 of our money, a part of which was to be paid at once, and hostages given for the remainder.

When the treaty was signed, Edward and his son immediately hastened to England. They then accompanied King John to Calais that the final conference with the *dauphin* might be held. After many more discussions, the peace was ratified. When all was arranged, and the hostages had arrived at Calais, who were to go to England till John's ransom was all paid, Edward gave a magnificent supper to King John in the castle. The king's sons, and all the greatest barons of England, waited bareheaded on the two kings. After the supper, Edward and John took leave of one another in the most affectionate manner. The Black Prince accompanied John to Boulogne. They went on foot, as the French king wished to make a pilgrimage to our Lady of Boulogne. There they met the *dauphin*, and all went together to the church and made their offerings, and afterwards to the abbey of Boulogne, where the Black Prince spent the day with the French, and returned next day to Calais. The English were not long in returning to England, taking with them all the French hostages.

Amongst these hostages were two sons of King John, the Dukes of Anjou and Berry, and his brother, the Duke of Orleans. Edward commanded his officers and courtiers to treat them courteously, and to be very careful to preserve peace with them, as they were under his care. They were allowed a great deal of liberty, and might go where they liked in the city of London and its neighbourhood. Froissart tells us that:

> They hunted and hawked according to their pleasure, and rode out as they pleased to visit the ladies without any constraint, for the king was right courteous and amiable.

The King of France was most joyfully welcomed by his subjects on his return. When he reached Paris, all the clergy came out to meet him, and conducted him to the palace, where he and his nobles partook of a magnificent dinner. So overjoyed were both people and nobles to see him, that they all made him rich gifts and entertained him at sumptuous feasts.

There was a good deal of difficulty in carrying out the articles of the treaty of Bretigny. Many of the French towns and strongholds which had to be given over to the English objected very strongly, and the King of France had to use much persuasion before they would consent to yield. The town of La Rochelle only yielded with difficulty, the principal inhabitants of the town saying, "We will honour and obey the English, but our hearts shall never change." On the other hand there were many small towns and fortresses in France which were held by English and Gascon nobles. These had to be given up to the King of France, and the soldiers who were turned out thought they could not better employ themselves than by forming themselves into robber bands, and pillaging the country. More than ever was France overrun by the free companies. The King of France was at last obliged to send an army against the largest of these companies, called the "Great Company;" but they defeated his army, and proceeded to threaten the Pope in Avignon, who was obliged to hire soldiers to oppose them.

Edward had appointed Sir John Chandos as regent and lieutenant of his possessions in France; and in the name of the King of England, Chandos received the homage of the nobles of Poitou, and the Duchy of Aquitaine. He made Niort his headquarters, and kept a great establishment there. He was a brave and accomplished knight, amiable and sweet-tempered, and was beloved and esteemed by the king, and all who knew him.

Chapter 11

Edward III.'s Jubilee

The Christmas after the treaty of Bretigny was spent by Edward and his court with great splendour at Woodstock. When the holidays were over, the king went to Winchester, where he had summoned his Parliament to meet him on the 24th of January, 1361. He told them all the articles of the peace concluded between him and the King of France, with which they expressed themselves entirely satisfied. On the last day of January the Archbishop of Canterbury celebrated the mass of the Holy Trinity in the presence of the court and Parliament, returning thanks for the peace. After the mass, torches were lighted and crosses held up over the Eucharist, the king and his sons standing up in the presence of the French hostages. Then all those lords who had not yet sworn to keep the peace took their oath, and signed a solemn declaration that they would observe all the conditions.

The Black Prince was now thirty-one years of age, and still unmarried. Struck, it is said, by the beauty of his cousin, Joan of Kent, he obtained the consent of his father to marry her. Joan was of the blood royal of England, being daughter of Edmund, Earl of Kent, son of Edward I. She had already been twice married, and was now a widow, and thirty-three years of age, somewhat older than the Black Prince. Her great beauty had won for her the name of the Fair Maid of Kent, and there is no reason to suppose that she had lost any of her charms at the time of her marriage to the Black Prince. The marriage took place on the 10th October, 1361, and in the following year, on the 14th July, Edward III. solemnly invested the Black Prince with the principality of Aquitaine and Gascony, giving him the title of Duke of Aquitaine.

The peace and prosperity of England was disturbed in 1362 by a second outbreak of the plague, which lasted from August till May. It was not so destructive as it had been the first time; but it seems to have been more fatal amongst the higher ranks of society. Amongst others, the king's cousin, the Duke of Lancaster, died of it. He left behind him only two daughters; the elder had been married to the Earl of Hainault, and the younger, Blanche, had married, in 1359, Edward's third son, John of Gaunt. Blanche, on the death of her elder sister, became heiress of all her father's great wealth, and it is in her right that John of Gaunt became Duke of Lancaster.

This marriage of John of Gaunt has a special interest to us, as it is said to have inspired one of Chaucer's earliest poems, the *Assembly of Foules; or, The Parliament of Birds*. The origin of the connexion between Chaucer and John of Gaunt is not known, but it seems to have begun early in the poet's life.

Geoffrey Chaucer was the son of a London vintner, and seems most probably to have been born in 1340. The facts of his early life are involved in obscurity, and we do not know whether his education was due to the wealth and enlightened views of his father, or to his having been early taken under royal patronage. John of Gaunt was never a popular man in English history, but he seems to have had the capacity of attracting to him the great literary characters of his age, for we know that both Chaucer and Wiclif were intimately connected with him.

Poetry had at that time become very fashionable, and was cultivated, more especially in France, by men of the highest rank. Chaucer therefore, though of humble birth, might hope to raise himself by his genius to be the friend even of a royal prince. If the date assigned to the *Assembly of Foules*, 1358, be a true one, it must rank as one of his earliest poems. He was then only eighteen years of age, but there are no signs of an unripe intellect about the poem. It is full of the freshness and life which always remained such distinguishing characteristics of Chaucer.

The poet has fallen asleep over his book, and he dreams that he is led into a beautiful park, "*walled with Green stone.*" With a few of his light, delicate touches he brings before us the whole scene, the "*trees clad with leaves that air shal last,*" the garden "*full of blossomed bow is;*" it is the orderly, sweet, fresh landscape that the medieval poet loved. At last he came to the spot where all the birds were gathered together before the noble goddess Nature, that, since it was Saint Valentine's day, each might choose his mate. Perched on Nature's hand was a beautiful female eagle, by whom the poet is supposed to have signified the Lady Blanche of Lancaster. Three eagles dispute vehemently as to which of them shall be her mate, and Nature refers the question to the assembly of birds. Each kind of bird chooses a representative to speak for them, and in the speeches of the different birds there is ample scope for Chaucer's playful humour and irony.

Characteristic of the spirit of chivalry is the great deference paid by the suitors to the lady herself. She is the "*soveraine lady,*" whom the royal eagle beseeches to be his "*through her mercy.*" No constraint is to be put on her choice, and Nature, as judge, decides that she shall have him on whom her heart is set. She bashfully asks for a year's respite in which to make her choice.

This charming little poem may almost be taken as a type of the excellencies of Chaucer. It shows us his love of nature, his vivacity, his humour. Like all that he has written, it reflects faithfully the spirit of his age, and breathes the very atmosphere of chivalry.

Chaucer was no doubt strongly influenced by the French Trouvères. Though first amongst the great English poets, he was an outcome of the poetic movement which had been going on for two centuries in the south of France and in Italy. He was the English representative of the great burst of medieval poetry, but came late in its development, and originated no great movement in England. He had some few successors and imitators; but after his death there is no great name in English literature till the revival of letters under the Tudors.

It is not difficult to see how French influences were brought to bear upon Chaucer. In those days there was constant intercourse between France and England. Chaucer himself went to France, as we have seen, with the royal army, in 1359, and remained there a year, till he was ransomed by Edward III. He also later on in his life visited Italy, and was intimately acquainted with the writings of Bocaccio and Petrarch, from whom he borrowed largely. But it was from the French Trouvères that he received his great impulse; he belonged to their school, and adopted their form and imagery. One of his first works was a translation of the *Romance of the Rose*. Yet he was no imitator. He was inspired by the spirit of the Trouvères, but everything he did is stamped with his own strong individuality, and has a decidedly English character. His greatest work, the *Canterbury Tales*, is most distinctively English.

He wrote another poem on the occasion of the death of the Duchess Blanche, in 1369, called the *Book of the Duchess*, in which he expresses the grief of the Duke of Lancaster. The setting of this poem is again quite in the character of the Trouvères. He employs his favourite machinery of a dream, which opens with the singing of birds on a May morning as

> *They sat along*
> *Upon my chamber roof without,*
> *Upon the tiles over all about,*
> *And songen everych in his wise*
> *The mosté solemné servise*
> *By note that ever man I trow*
> *Had heard.*

He gives us an interesting picture of a medieval room by describing that in which he lay. It was painted all over with frescoes illustrating the Romance of the Rose, and the windows were filled with beautiful painted glass, on which was wrought the history of the siege of Troy. As he lies in bed he hears the sound of a horn, and jumps up that he may follow the hunt. Then, as he wanders through the wood, he comes upon a knight sitting mourning at the foot of an oak tree. This of course is John of Gaunt who with bitter tears deplores the death of his lady.

Chaucer continued all through his life to find a powerful friend in John of Gaunt. To his influence he doubtless owed various offices, which he held at different times. He was several times sent abroad on secret affairs of state, and at last obtained a permanent office in London, with a salary, and besides had a pension granted to him. His connexion with John of Gaunt was strengthened by the fact that his wife's sister, Katherine Swynford, who had been in the service of the Duchess Blanche, first became the duke's mistress, and afterwards his third wife.

The advantage of such a patron to the poet must have been great, as it relieved him from all anxiety about money, and permitted him to devote most of his energy to his art.

We cannot overestimate what Chaucer did for the English language. Before his time French was the common language of the court, the schools, the law courts, and all the higher classes of society. The dialects spoken in different parts of England differed widely from one another, and it remained a question which of these dialects should triumph and form the cultivated English language. It was Chaucer who decided this question. It was his language that was to become the standard of English. This was due to the force of his genius, which made men feel the beauty, the power, and the capacities of the language which he used, so that insensibly it became the language of all cultivated men. And as the English language developed, it triumphed over the French. One of the acts, which commemorated Edward III.'s jubilee, is an edict in which he said, that as the French tongue *"was much unknown in the country,"* all pleas should be henceforth in English.

On the 14th November, 1362, Edward III. celebrated his jubilee; that is, his fiftieth birthday. In honour of the day he proclaimed a general pardon, and set all prisoners at liberty, and recalled all exiles. To commemorate it still further, he conferred various dignities upon his sons. Lionel was made Duke of Clarence; John of Gaunt was solemnly raised to the dignity of Duke of Lancaster. The king in full Parliament girt him with a sword, and set upon his head a cap of fur, and a circlet of gold and pearls. Edmund, the fourth son, was made Earl of Cambridge.

This was the climax of Edward's prosperity. On his fiftieth birthday he might look back upon his life, and say that fortune had indeed favoured him; but from henceforth things did not go so well. Misfortunes and troubles marked the last years of his life, and in the end he was destined to lose almost all that he had won. It is not difficult to see how this came about. Edward III. was a brave and accomplished knight, a man full of energy and interests, anxious to protect commerce and manufacture, to increase the wealth of his people, and to win glory for himself by his wars; but he had no great purpose in his life.

He collected mighty armies, at an enormous expense, and led them into the enemy's country without any definite scheme of what he meant to do. His own bravery and that of his soldiers enabled him to win great victories; but not content with grasping firmly what he had once got, he indulged in an ambitious dream of one day winning the crown of France. Even when the peace of Bretigny had secured to him the great Duchy of Aquitaine, neither he nor the Black Prince had sufficient political wisdom to take such steps as would have preserved it for the English Crown. They had won it, but they could not keep it.

Over the joy of Edward's jubilee there hung no shadow of distrust for the future. The next year the Black Prince was to go and take up his abode in his new Duchy of Aquitaine, and the months before his departure were filled up with hunting parties in the royal forests, which were conducted with the greatest possible magnificence, and with no sparing of expense. The king and queen, with their children, spent Christmas at the Black Prince's manor of Berkhampstead, near London. Here were many jousts and tournaments, and all the usual Christmas games and festivities.

The general extravagance and love of dress must have increased to an alarming extent; for the next year is marked by a sumptuary statute, which aimed at diminishing extravagance and high prices. It decreed that each merchant was to deal only with one sort of merchandise, which he must choose before the feast of Candlemas. Handicraftsmen also were to practise only one "mystery," as the trades were then called, exceptions only being allowed in the case of women workers. The goldsmiths were to make their work sterling, and each master goldsmith was to have his own mark. His work must be assayed by the royal surveyors, who were to put the king's mark on it, and then the goldsmith was to put his own mark. No goldsmith might make both gold and silver plate. The prices at which he was to sell his work were fixed.

The statute went on to regulate matters of mere personal expenditure. It ordained that the poor were "to eat and drink in the manner that pertaineth to them, and not excessively;" that they were not to eat fish or meat more than once a day. "Seeing that various people wore clothing above their estate and degree," it ordained that the handicraftsmen and yeomen were not to wear cloth above a certain price, and no silk and embroidery, ribands or gold and silver ornaments. The ploughmen and all agricultural labourers were only to wear tunics of blanket or russet, with girdles of linen. Above all, no one except persons of the highest rank was to wear fur or pearls.

The statute was not prompted by any feeling of the evils of luxury amongst the ruling classes. About the time of its promulgation Archbishop Simon Islip issued a "Remonstrance against the abuses, the foppery, and extravagance of the court." The upper classes had no intention of reforming their own extravagance; but they wished to have the monopoly of all luxuries, and they fancied that the more extensive use of fine clothes and various kinds of victuals greatly increased their price. These sumptuary laws show with what bitter jealousy the nobility regarded the growing wealth and prosperity of the merchant classes.

The burghers of London were indeed becoming very rich and powerful. About this time Henry Picard, a vintner, the Lord Mayor of London, sumptuously feasted Edward III., the Black Prince, David

Bruce (King of Scotland), the King of Cyprus (who had come to ask Edward's help against the Turks), and many nobles. Afterwards he kept open house to any who liked to play at dice or hazard with him, whilst his wife, the Lady Margaret, received the ladies in her upper room.

The King of Cyprus engaged in play with Picard, and won fifty *marks*; but Picard was a good player, and soon won back more than he had lost, at which the king was much vexed. He tried to hide his irritation; but Picard saw it, and said to him, "My lord king, be not aggrieved, I covet not your gold but your play, for I have not bid you hither that I might grieve you, but that, amongst other things, I might try your play." Then he gave him his money back again, and distributed more among his servants. He gave also many rich gifts to Edward III., his son, and the knights who had dined with them.

At a later period the city bought a large quantity of plate to present to the Black Prince, at a cost of £683 10s. 4d., which equals about £10,252 of our money, (as at time of first publication). Amongst other articles, all of silver, were ten dozen porringers, five dozen saltcellars, and twenty chargers. There were also three gilded basins, six gilded pots, a gilded cup in the form of an acorn, and a pair of ivory bottles. The total number of articles was 279.

Not only amongst the people at large, but still more at the English court itself, had extravagance in dress and manner of living increased at an enormous rate. Old English simplicity was more than ever forgotten, and large sums of money were wasted on every side merely on display in matters of food and clothing.

The remonstrance of Archbishop Islip attracted some attention, but produced as little effect on the fashions of the day as did the sumptuary laws just passed by Parliament. Display was characteristic of Edward; and where the king set the example it was only likely that the people would follow. The mass of the clergy were worse than the people. They who ought to have set an example of greater sobriety and simplicity, were especially renowned for their love of good eating and fine clothes. Whilst they followed the chase, and gave themselves up to pleasure of every kind, they left their people wandering as flocks without shepherds.

A noticeable event occurred in the year 1362. Some of the French hostages had begun to weary of their confinement, and asked Edward's permission to go to Calais and make some excursions into the surrounding country, promising never to be absent for more than four days at a time. The king, believing that he might trust their promise, granted their request; but the Duke of Anjou basely took advantage of this permission to break his parole, and went off to Paris. His father, King John, was so deeply grieved at this breach of faith that he determined to go back himself to England as a prisoner in the place of his son who had escaped.

The English received him with great respect and courtesy, and he took up his abode again at the Savoy Palace. Edward did all he could to make his captivity pleasant; but he was seized with a mortal sickness, and died three months after his return to England.

CHAPTER 12

The Black Prince in Aquitaine

When the Black Prince had been created Duke of Aquitaine, the barons and knights of that country were very anxious that he should come and live amongst them, and they often entreated the king that he would allow him to do so. The English Parliament also, seeing the large sums of money which were necessary to keep up the magnificent establishments of the king and his sons in England, represented to Edward that if the Black Prince were to set up his court in Aquitaine, that rich and fertile country would supply all his expenses. The Black Prince himself was nothing loath to go there, and set to work to make the necessary preparations for his journey. His wife was to accompany him, as well as many English barons and knights, and he intended to establish his court in Aquitaine with all the magnificence of an independent prince.

Aquitaine had been now for more than two hundred years in the hands of the English, and some of the English kings had given a good deal of attention to means for promoting the prosperity of the country. Edward I. had begun a course of policy which, if it had been continued, might have done much to strengthen the ties which bound Aquitaine to England. He had founded many new towns, which he endowed with special privileges, so as to induce inhabitants to flock to them. As these towns owned no intermediate lord, and owed all their privileges to the English Crown, the inhabitants naturally regarded the English rule with favour. Edward I.'s towns were all built on a regular plan, and to this day are sometimes called English towns.

When founded, they were called *bastides*. They had two parallel streets at a short distance from one another, connected by many short narrow lanes. In the middle of the town was the market-place, in one corner of which stood the church. Here was the market-hall, with a great weighing machine to weigh the merchandise; here also was the well or fountain of the town. The houses round the marketplace, as was the custom in southern climates, were built on arcades, which protected the merchants from the hot rays of the sun whilst conducting their business. In fifty years, fifty of these towns had been founded. Many of them were named after the English officers who superintended their foundation. Charters were given them, and as they were free towns and had no over-lord, they were regarded with great jealousy by the other towns. Libourne was the most important and flourishing of these *bastides*, and excited the jealousy of Bordeaux itself. Edward III. renewed its charters, and further allowed its inhabitants to have free trade with England, releasing them from all custom dues at Bordeaux.

At the death of Edward I. the English ceased to found *bastides*; but they carried on a policy likely to be equally successful in winning the affections of the people. They annexed to the crown a large number of towns, freeing them from their over-lords, and granting them charters. This freedom from over-lords was what all the towns in the middle ages were struggling to get. As the towns had grown up on land belonging to some baron, they owed him, like other inferior vassals, certain dues and money payments. They had no corporate and independent existence until they could obtain a charter of liberties from their over-lord. The struggle of towns to obtain charters was going on in all countries during the course of the middle ages. As a rule the monarchs favoured the towns, hoping thereby to get their support and aid in their own struggles against the nobles.

Edward III. committed a mistake by departing from the policy of his predecessors, and giving back many of the towns in Aquitaine to the chief Gascon lords, who belonged to the English party. He was anxious by this means to win the aid of the nobles in his wars against France, but he forgot that if he wished to keep any permanent hold on the Duchy of Aquitaine he must secure the affections of the people. The nobles were ready to fight for anyone who would give them wealth and sufficient opportunities for plunder, and France might easily outbid Edward. The people could only be won by a wise and liberal government. The towns could not hope for much from Edward. They saw him disregard their dearest wishes and interests, and give them back into the hands of their over-lords.

Aquitaine must have presented a flourishing appearance when the Black Prince arrived to take up his abode there. The rich and fertile country was covered with vineyards, and the *bastides* of Edward I., with their regular streets and fine market-places, had increased into flourishing towns. The wine trade with England was carried on very vigorously; though here as in many other cases Edward III.'s over-busy legislation was a hindrance rather than a benefit. At one time he would allow no English merchants to go to Gascony to buy wine, but enacted that all the wine must be brought to England by Gascon merchants. When complaints were raised that large quantities of wine lay unsold in Aquitaine for want of English buyers, he revoked his prohibition, but forbade the English merchants to carry the wine to any other country but England. The Black Prince drew most of his revenue from the duties on wine, so that it was of no small importance to him that the trade should flourish.

The Black Prince with his wife, the Princess Joan, and all his followers, arrived at de Rochelle in the beginning of the year 1363. Here they were met by Sir John Chandos, who had come from Niort to receive them. He was followed by a large number of knights and squires, who all greeted the prince with great joy. They spent four days at Rochelle in feastings and merriment, and then went to Poitiers, where the prince received the homage of all the knights of Poitou and Saintonge. Then he rode on to Bordeaux, and at every city on his way the knights and barons crowded to do him homage.

At Bordeaux he and his wife established their court, and received all the nobles of Aquitaine who came to pay him their respects. The court at Bordeaux was very brilliant. The prince had his father's love for feasting and fine clothes. Splendid merry-making was the fashion of the age, and life at the Black Prince's court was a succession of revels and tournaments. He was a right noble host, and knew how to make all around him happy. Chandos the Herald says:

> Never since the birth of Christ was there such good and honourable entertainment. Every day at his table he had more than eighty knights, and four times as many esquires. There they made jousts and revels. Though all of them were subjects, yet were they all free; for he made them quite welcome. All who were about his person valued and loved him; for liberality was his staff, and nobleness his director. Rightly might men say, that search the whole world you could find no such prince.

It is no wonder that the Gascon lords crowded to this court. Even the greatest of them all, the Counts of Foix and Armagnac, came to visit him, and they found that his court was as splendid as that of the King of France himself.

But we must not let our eyes be dazzled by all this magnificence. To meet the expenses of his court the Prince allowed the resources of the country to be drained. Though we may admire his noble hospitality and his princely courtesy to all comers, we cannot altogether consider him a wise governor. His mind seems only to have been occupied with the desire of making his court gay and pleasant, instead of furthering the true interests of the people whom he was called upon to govern. Here again he may be taken as a type of his age. We must not judge him by any standard of our own, but by the standard of his days. But the time was fast coming when it would be no longer possible for the rulers to forget the interests of the people, when the people would at last succeed in making their voice heard; and we shall see that at the end of his days the Black Prince did not refuse to hear them.

In 1364 there were great rejoicings at the birth of the prince's first son Edward. This little prince only lived to be seven years old: but in 1366 the Princess of Wales bore another son, called Richard of Bordeaux from his birthplace, who ruled England as Richard II.

The prince had not long set up his court at Bordeaux before it seemed likely that peace would again be disturbed. In his new dominions he had become the neighbour of Spain, and he was now called upon to interfere in Spanish affairs.

Up to this time Spain had been of little importance in the general affairs of Europe. The energies of its people had been entirely spent in fighting one long crusade against their Moorish conquerors. The disunion between the small Christian kingdoms long hindered their success against the Moors. But in 1230 the Christian kingdoms of Castile and Leon were united under one ruler, who, being wise and powerful, succeeded in winning back a large territory from the Moslem. The Kings of Portugal and Aragon had also been successful in the west and east of the peninsula, and at last nothing was left of the Mahometan power in Spain save the kingdom of Grenada.

It is easy to understand, that whilst the kingdoms of Spain were disunited, and were engaged in this desperate struggle against the Moors, on which their very existence as a nation depended, they had no time to interfere in the affairs of Europe, and except for the connexion of the Kings of Aragon with Naples and Sicily, remained almost entirely outside European politics.

Now, however, things were more settled in Spain. It was divided into five kingdoms, the four Christian kingdoms of Castile, Aragon, Portugal, and Navarre, and the Mahometan kingdom of Grenada. Of these Castile was the largest, and had, from its neighbourhood to the Duchy of Aquitaine, been connected with the Kings of England. A daughter of Henry II. of England had been married to the King of Castile, and Edward I. had married Eleanor of Castile, who had known well how to gain the love and veneration of the English people. As Dukes of Aquitaine, it was the policy of the English kings to be on friendly terms with the Kings of Castile. Contending commercial interests had provoked discord from time to time, as we have seen in speaking of the great sea fight of Winchelsea, when Edward III. defeated the fleet of the maritime cities of Biscay; but this was in no way a quarrel between the two monarchs, and their friendly relations remained unchanged.

So it happened that when the King of Castile, Don Pedro, was chased from his throne on account of his cruelty and tyranny, he turned naturally to the Black Prince, hoping to find in him a friend. He had been engaged to marry the prince's sister, the Princess Joan, who had died of the plague at Bordeaux on her way to Spain. He called himself therefore the prince's brother-in-law, and considered that he had a claim to the prince's friendship.

This Don Pedro was cruel and wicked, and by his tyranny had gained the hatred of his subjects. He had caused many of the proudest Spanish nobles to be secretly assassinated or executed for some pretended crime, and had even caused the death of his own wife, who was a French princess. Moreover, he was regarded with abhorrence by the Pope, because he oppressed the Church, and lived on friendly terms with the Moorish King of Grenada. The Pope therefore legitimatised his bastard brother, Henry of Trastamare, a bold and valiant knight, and encouraged him to wrest the kingdom from Don Pedro.

Henry had special reasons to hate Don Pedro; for one of the tyrant's first victims had been Henry's mother, Leonora de Guzman; and it was only with difficulty that Henry himself, and his brother Don Tello, had escaped from Pedro's hands, when he seized and executed the other members of their family.

Neither was it difficult for Henry of Trastamare to find friends and supporters. Within his own dominions Pedro had no friends; and in Charles V., who had been King of France since the death of his father King John, Henry found a ready ally.

Charles had various reasons for animosity to Pedro. He resented bitterly the murder of his kinswoman, Pedro's queen, and saw in Pedro an ally of England. Charles V. was a wise and cautious man. Though he writhed under the burdensome obligations of the peace of Bretigny, he felt that he was not yet strong enough to reopen the war with England. Now he hoped that, by aiding Henry of Trastamare, he might strike a blow at the English power through their ally.

Another important reason influenced him in this direction. France, as we have seen, was devastated by the Free Companies, who were daily growing more powerful. The Pope at Avignon trembled before them, and it was equally important to both Charles V. and the Pope to get rid of them. The two therefore joined together in hiring these companies to aid Henry. A treaty was concluded with the leaders of the companies, who were only too glad to engage on a military expedition in which they might hope for plenteous spoils. The French general, Bertrand Du Guesclin, whose fame had grown in the Breton war, was ransomed from captivity in Britany, that he might lead the Free Companies into Spain. Amongst the chiefs of the companies were many English and Gascons, who went in spite of Edward III.'s commands to the contrary. They marched over the Pyrenees into Spain, and were met at Barcelona by Henry of Trastamare.

There was no one found to take up the cause of the hated Pedro, who lost his throne without a battle, and was obliged to fly, with his two daughters, to the fortress of Corunna, and then to Bayonne. Thence he sent letters to the Black Prince, asking for his protection and aid.

We may be surprised that the Black Prince listened for a moment to the entreaties of a man whose own crimes had lost him his throne, and whose wickedness drew on him universal abhorrence. But, on the other hand, there were many things which recommended Pedro to his pity. He was the ally of England, and as a helpless fugitive asked for aid; it was always the part of a true knight to succour the distressed. Again, there was a very strong feeling in favour of the legitimate sovereign, however great his crimes might be; and we cannot wonder at one ruler feeling sympathy for the misfortunes of another. The whole situation appealed strongly to the chivalric spirit of the prince. As a Christian knight, it was his duty, without any further thought of policy, to receive the fugitive hospitably, and help him to win back his rightful inheritance.

Some motives of policy also came in to influence him. Should an ally of France be placed on the throne of Castile, the Black Prince would be awkwardly placed in Aquitaine, with a declared enemy on one side, and a probable enemy on the other. Possibly also he indulged in some hope that he might get substantial advantages from aiding Pedro, and that he might even be able to annex the maritime province of Biscaya, with all its thriving commercial cities, whose spirit of enterprise led them to compete even with England herself.

Still the policy which could lead the Black Prince to help Pedro was not very far-sighted. He might have seen that it would be impossible to establish firmly on the throne a ruler so much hated as was Pedro. In the end the opposite party must triumph, and then he would find that he had embittered them against himself by helping their enemy. His wisest course would have been to do all in his power to secure the friendship of Henry of Trastamare; but this was opposed to all his feelings of what was due to an ally in distress.

On receiving Don Pedro's letters, the Black Prince immediately sent for Sir John Chandos and Sir William Felton, his chief advisers, and said to them, smiling, "My lords, here is great news from Spain." He then told them what he had heard, and begged them to tell him frankly what they thought he ought to do. They advised him to send a body of soldiers to bring Don Pedro safely to Bayonne, that they might learn his condition from his own mouth. Their advice pleased the prince, and he sent Sir William Felton and a number of other knights to fetch Don Pedro. They met him at Bayonne, and treating him with the utmost honour, brought him to Bordeaux.

The prince rode out of the town at the head of his knights to meet the fugitive king. He greeted him respectfully, and led him into the city with great courtesy. An apartment had been prepared for him, and in all things he was treated with the honour due to a reigning sovereign. Feasts and tournaments were held, and everything was done which could make him forget his miserable condition. Don Pedro on his side did all he could to attach the prince to his interests. He had nothing but promises to give, and of these he was most liberal, promising rich gifts of money and lands to the prince, and all his knights, if they would help his cause.

There were not wanting wise men amongst the prince's counsellors to dissuade him from giving Don Pedro any help. They spoke to him of his secure and prosperous condition, telling him that he could want for nothing more, and that to try for more might endanger what he already possessed. They showed him the unworthiness of Pedro, how he was an enemy to religion, had oppressed his subjects, and was hated by all men. But all this made no impression on the prince. He could not shut his eyes to Don Pedro's distress, nor forget that he had come as a fugitive to ask his help. Before deciding upon anything, however, he assembled a great council of all the barons of his duchy to ask their advice. Many of the council were eager for the enterprise, as knights in those days longed for anything which might win them honour. They agreed, however, to send ambassadors to England, to ask the advice of the king.

When the answer came back, it appeared that Edward III. and his council were clearly of the same opinion as the prince. They advised him to aid Don Pedro with all the force at his command. The expedition was determined upon; but next arose the question of payment. The barons of Aquitaine were not willing to engage in this enterprise at their own expense. Don Pedro assured the prince that there need be no difficulty on this head; once restored to the throne of Castile, he would have abundant treasure at his command, and would pay all the expenses of the war. The Black Prince put such trust in his word, that he made himself answerable for the expenses of the war, believing that Pedro would not fail to pay him. Chandos and Felton, however, advised the prince to melt down some of his plate, of which he possessed an enormous quantity, for immediate expenses. Swords and coats of mail were forged at Bordeaux in preparation for the expedition.

Letters were sent to the leaders of the English Free Companies, who had accompanied Henry of Trastamare into Spain, bidding them return and aid in this expedition. It was a matter of perfect indifference to these companies for whom they fought, provided they had pay and booty enough. Though they had helped Henry of Trastamare to the throne, they were quite willing to serve under the banner of the Black Prince, and to pull down in turn the king whom they had set up.

It was necessary to obtain permission from the King of Navarre to pass through his dominions, which lay between Aquitaine and Castile. Charles the Bad had pledged himself to Henry of Trastamare not to let any troops pass through his kingdom; but he was soon persuaded by the promise of a large sum of money to break his word.

Chapter 13

Spanish Campaign

The troops were to collect at Dax for the expedition. The Black Prince did his utmost to attach the Free Companies firmly to him, by distributing amongst them the money which he had raised by melting down his plate. His father, learning his want of money, had consented to send him the yearly payment made by the French in consideration of the sum of money still due for King John's ransom. This money also was distributed amongst the companies.

On Wednesday, the feast of the Epiphany, when the Black Prince's preparations for leaving Bordeaux were already complete, he was rejoiced by the birth of his son Richard. He stayed to see his child baptized by the Archbishop of Bordeaux, and on the following day his wife had to take leave of him. She was filled with anxiety at his departure, as the expedition was considered to be full of danger; and the herald Chandos tells us that she bitterly lamented his departure, saying:

> Alas! what will happen to me if I shall lose the true flower of gentleness, the flower of magnanimity—him who in the world has no equal to be named for courage? I have no heart, no blood, no veins, but every member fails me when I think of his departure.

But when the prince heard her lamentation he comforted her, and said, "Lady, cease your lament, and be not dismayed; for God is able to do all things." Then he took his leave of her very tenderly, and said lovingly, "Lady, we shall meet again in such case, that we shall have joy, both we and all our friends; for my heart tells me this." Then they embraced with many tears, and all the dames and damsels of the court wept also, some weeping for their lovers, some for their husbands.

The prince and his knights left Bordeaux on January 10th, and went to Dax, where the troops were collecting. A few days afterwards, the prince's brother, John of Gaunt, Duke of Lancaster, arrived at Bordeaux with a body of troops which he had brought from England to aid in the expedition. He was welcomed with great joy by the princess and her ladies. He would not stay, however, but pressed on to Dax, where his brother waited his coming. Froissart tells us that the two brothers were very happy in this meeting, for they had much affection for each other; and many proofs of affection passed between them and their men.

Meanwhile Henry of Trastamare had not been idle in preparing for this invasion. All Spain was on his side, and the French king had sent troops to his assistance under his general, Bertrand du Guesclin. Much romance has been woven round the history of this famous man, who was to be the arm by which Charles V. should free himself from the English, and who himself, at one time the leader of a free company, was to deliver France from the scourge of the companies. It is difficult in the story of his life to separate truth from romance. He was a Breton, and in those days it was said that none in France were good soldiers except the Bretons and the Gascons. His origin is obscure, and he is supposed to have been the son of a peasant. Even his most enthusiastic admirers allow him to have been a rough, rude man, extremely ugly, of middle height, with a dark complexion and green eyes, long arms and large shoulders.

As a tactician, he was far in advance of such simple soldiers as Edward III. and the Black Prince. He had advanced beyond the ideas of chivalry, where the one aim was to fight bravely. He preferred to win by cunning, if possible, and did not care how often he broke his plighted word. He was one of a new race of soldiers, who sought to win by tactics rather than by hard fighting, to avoid a battle rather than risk one. Still, if it were necessary to fight, he was always foremost, and knew no fear. He gave no quarter, and thirsted for revenge against his foes. The characteristic way in which he always plunged into the thickest of the battle without thinking of his own safety, is shown by the fact that he was twice in his life taken prisoner. When he had money he was prodigal of it, but he was at all times eager for booty and pillage. He had fought with success in Britany against De Montfort and the English, and was now ready to measure his strength with the most renowned captain of his age, the Black Prince.

Charles V., King of France, to whom history has given the name of the Wise, only complied with the conditions of the peace of Bretigny, that time might strengthen his resources, whilst it weakened those of his enemies. Not a brave soldier himself—in the Battle of Poitiers he was one of those who first sought safety in flight—he had no ambition to command his own armies as the other monarchs of his age had done; but his wisdom had made him lay his hand upon Du Guesclin, as the fit person to be his general.

In spite of the agreement which the English had made with the King of Navarre, they were still afraid of him, for they heard that he had again begun to treat with Henry of Trastamare. The Black Prince ordered two of the frontier towns of Navarre to be invested with English troops, and compelled the King of Navarre to accompany the army until it had safely passed through his dominions. They crossed the Pyrenees by the pass of Roncesvalles. The passage through these narrow defiles was most dangerous and difficult, as it was now the middle of winter. The entire army was almost overwhelmed by a frightful snowstorm, which overtook them in the mountains. They suffered great loss both in men and beasts, but at last reached the valley of Pampeluna, where they stopped to recruit their forces.

Whilst they were waiting there, the King of Navarre, as he was riding about, was taken prisoner by a French captain. He was supposed to have purposely allowed this to happen, that he might be freed from all further personal responsibility as to the war. One of his knights however conducted the Prince through the kingdom of Navarre, and provided guides for the army through the difficult mountain roads. The army crossed the deep and rapid Ebro by the bridge at Logrono, and encamped near the little town of Navarette. Don Henry and Du Guesclin were not far off, encamped near Najera on the little River Najerilla.

From Navarette the Black Prince sent his manifesto to Don Henry. In this he stated that he had come to restore the legitimate king to his throne, and expressed his amazement that Henry, who had sworn allegiance to his brother, should have ventured afterwards to take up arms against him, and drive him from his rightful throne. He called God and St. George to witness that he was willing even now to settle the dispute by mediation; but if that were refused, there was nothing left for it but to fight. Henry answered on the following day. He said that the whole kingdom had fallen away from Don Pedro, and attached themselves to him; that it was heaven's doing, and no one had a right to interfere. He also, in God's name and St. Iago's, had no desire for a battle; but he forbade the enemy to press any further into his country.

On their march to Logrono, the prince's army had suffered much from want of provisions; he was therefore eager for a battle as soon as possible; but the enemy waited to attack till all their troops should have arrived. Sir William Felton went with a body of men to reconnoitre the enemy, but was attacked by a large number of French and Spaniards, and was slain, after a most valiant fight. Sir Hugh Calverly, another of the bravest English knights, was also surprised and slain by a large body of Spaniards, who had gone out under Don Tello, Henry's brother, to reconnoitre the English Army.

These successes filled the Spaniards with joy and confidence. Henry said to his brother, "I will reward you handsomely for this; and I feel that all the rest of our enemies must at last come to this pass." But on this one of the French knights spoke up, and bade him not be too confident; for with the Black Prince was the flower of chivalry of the whole world, all hardy and tough combatants, who would die rather than think of flying. "But," he added, "if you follow my advice, you can take them all without striking a blow." He then advised Henry simply to keep watch over all the passes and defiles, so that no provisions could be brought to the English Army, and when famine had done its work, to attack them as they retreated.

This advice was very sound, and would doubtless have been successful if it had been followed; but Henry was far too impetuous a knight to be content to pursue a policy of inaction. He crossed the little river Najerilla with his army, and spread out his forces in a beautiful open plain, which was broken neither by tree nor bush for a great distance. The army was divided into three battalions, and their front was covered by men who threw stones with slings. When all were formed in order, Henry mounted a handsome mule and rode through the ranks, exhorting and encouraging the men.

The Black Prince meanwhile was not very far off. The previous night he had been encamped at a distance of only two leagues from the enemy, and was now marching to meet him in full battle array. He crossed a hill to reach the plain where Henry's army lay, and advanced down a long, deep valley. The sun was just rising when the two armies came in sight of one another, and it was a beautiful sight, says Froissart, to see the battalions as they advanced to meet, their brilliant armour glittering in the sunbeams.

The prince mounted a hill, that he might see the Spaniards; and after observing them, ordered his army to halt, and spread out in line of battle. Immediately before the battle he raised Sir John Chandos to the rank of a knight banneret, to the great joy of those knights and squires who fought under Sir John.

Then the prince spoke a few words to the army:

> Today, sirs, has, as you well know, no other termination but in famine. For want of food we are well-nigh taken. See, there are our enemies, who have food enough—bread and wine, and fish, salt and fresh, from the river and the sea. These we must now obtain by dint of lance and sword. Now let us do such a day's work that we may part from our foes with honour.

Then he knelt down, and prayed:

> O very Sovereign Father, who hast made and fashioned us, so truly as Thou knowest that I am not come hither but to defend the right, for prowess and for liberty, that my heart leaps and burns to obtain a life of honour, I pray Thee that on this day Thou wilt guard me and my people.

After which he rose, and exclaimed, "Advance, banners; God defend the right." Then, turning to Don Pedro, he took him by the hand, and said, "Certainly, Sir King, today you shall know if ever you shall recover Castile; have firm trust in God."

Then the battle began. The first battalion of the English Army, commanded by John of Gaunt and Chandos, engaged the French contingent of the Spanish Army, commanded by Du Guesclin. John of Gaunt encouraged his men, shouting, "Advance, banners, advance! let us take God to our rescue, and each to his honour." Meanwhile the prince, near whom rode Don Pedro, attacked the second division of the Spanish Army, commanded by Don Tello. At the first encounter the Spanish troops were seized with terror, and fled in wild confusion, so that the prince was at liberty to engage the main body of the enemy, commanded by Henry. Here the Spaniards, encouraged by the presence of their king, fought with much greater bravery. The stones, thrown with great force from the slings of the Spanish foot soldiers, did much harm to their opponents, and many were unhorsed by them; but the English arrows "flew straighter than rain in winter time," and the Spanish cavalry began to break before them.

Thrice Henry rallied his men; but at last it was hopeless, and he was obliged to fly. Du Guesclin and his French soldiers also gave the

Dukes of Lancaster and Chandos plenty to do. Chandos was unhorsed, and only saved his life by his great coolness and presence of mind. The French knights bore themselves most valiantly. Du Guesclin, who would never fly, even though he saw the day was lost, was surrounded and taken prisoner.

The Spaniards and French fled across the river to the town of Najara. Many were killed in crossing the bridge; so that the river was dyed red with the blood of men and horses. The English and Gascons entered the town with them, and took many of the knights, and killed many of the people. In Henry's lodgings they found much plate and jewels; for he had come there with great splendour.

The English victory was complete. At noon the battle was over, and the Black Prince ordered his banner to be fixed in a bush on a little height, as a rallying-point for his men on their return from the pursuit. The Duke of Lancaster and others among the knights did the same, and the men soon gathered round the different banners in good order. The prince bade that they should look among the dead for the body of Henry of Trastamare, and also discover what men of rank had been slain. He then descended, with Don Pedro and his knights, to King Henry's lodgings. Here they found plenty of every sort, at which they rejoiced greatly; for they had suffered great want before. When the men returned from searching the battlefield, Don Pedro was much displeased at hearing that his brother was not among the slain. The slaughter had been very great amongst the common soldiers. Besides those lying dead on the battlefield, many were drowned in the river.

That night the army rested in ease and luxury, enjoying plenty of food and wine. Next morning, which was Palm Sunday, Pedro's mind was already full of thoughts of revenge. He came to the prince, and asked that he would give up to him all the Spanish prisoners, the traitors of his country, that he might cut off their heads. But the prince answered him—

> Sir King, I entreat and beg of you to pardon all the ill which your rebellious subjects have done against you. Thus you will do an act of kindness and generosity, and will remain in peace in your kingdom.

Pedro was not in a position to refuse the prince's request, since he owed everything to him, and he had to pardon all the Spanish nobles, excepting one, who in some manner had earned his special anger, and whom the prince gave up to him. He was beheaded in front of Don

Pedro's tent, before his very eyes.

The next day the army set out on its march toward Burgos, and the citizens, who knew that resistance was useless, opened their gates to Don Pedro. The prince and his army encamped in the plain outside the town, as there were not comfortable quarters for them all inside. Here the return of Don Pedro was celebrated with tournaments, banquets, and processions; and the Black Prince presided as judge over all the tournaments. All Castile yielded to Don Pedro, and the Black Prince might congratulate himself that he had done his work speedily and well. He exhorted Pedro on every occasion to treat his people well, and pardon their revolt from his rule, saying to him:

> I advise you for your good, if you would be King of Castile, that you send forth word that you have consented to give pardon to all those who have been against you.

Pedro promised everything he asked; and as long as the Black Prince stayed by his side, he did not dare to indulge his desire for vengeance.

But when the prince had been a month at Burgos, he began to be impatient to return to his own dominions. He had as yet received none of the promised money from Pedro, in payment of the expenses of the campaign. He therefore told the king that he was anxious to return and disband his army, and demanded the money to pay his troops. Pedro said that he fully intended to pay as he had promised, but that at that moment he had no money. At Seville, however, he had a large treasure, and if the Black Prince would allow him to depart, he would go and fetch it. Meanwhile, he proposed that the prince and his army should quarter themselves in the fertile country round Valladolid. He promised to bring him the money at Whitsuntide. The Black Prince, himself always honest and straightforward, was ever ready to trust in others, and easily agreed to do as Pedro proposed. It was a fatal step; for once away from Pedro's side, he lost all hold upon him.

The prince's army established itself round Valladolid, and the Free Companies supported themselves by pillaging the peasants. The summer drew on, and the army began to suffer from the hot climate. Disease broke out in the camp, and it is said that four out of every five of the soldiers died. Whitsuntide came, but brought no money from Pedro. The prince grew more and more uneasy. At last he sent three of his knights to the Spanish king, to ask him why he did not keep his promise. To them Pedro professed great sorrow that he had not been able to send the money sooner, and repeated his promises; but said that he could not drain his people of money, and, above all, he could not send any money as long as the Free Companies were in the country; for they did so much harm. If the prince would send the companies away, and only let some of his knights remain, he would soon send the money.

When this answer was brought back to the prince he became very sad; for he saw clearly that Don Pedro did not mean to keep his promises. His own health was failing; he had been attacked by an illness which was never to leave him. Bad news was brought him from Bordeaux. The princess wrote that Henry of Trastamare was attacking the frontiers of Aquitaine. His army was rapidly dwindling before his eyes. Man after man died from the effects of the climate. There was nothing for it but to return to Bordeaux. In sadness he gathered his troops together, and felt thankful that he was allowed to pass peaceably through Navarre and the dangerous passes of the Pyrenees.

At Bayonne he disbanded his army, now only a miserable remnant of the magnificent array of troops which he had led into Spain. He bade them come to Bordeaux to receive the payment due to them. He said to them, that though Don Pedro had not kept his engagements, it did not become him to act in like manner to those who had served him so well. On his arrival at Bordeaux he was received with solemn processions, the priests coming out to meet him, bearing crosses. The princess followed, with her eldest son Edward, then three years old, surrounded by her ladies and knights. They were full of joy at meeting one another again, and embraced most tenderly, and then walked together hand in hand to their abode. Soon after the prince assembled all the nobles of Aquitaine, who had joined in this expedition, thanked them heartily for their help, and distributed among them rich presents of gold and silver, and jewels.

CHAPTER 14

Failure in Aquitaine

Though crowned with success, the Spanish expedition was most fatal in its consequences to the Black Prince. His victory in Spain had caused him to be esteemed as the greatest among the princes and generals of Europe. The news of it had been received in England with enthusiastic joy; bonfires, rejoicings, and thanksgivings in the churches had celebrated it all over the country. But what was the result? The Prince had restored for a moment a bloodthirsty tyrant to the throne, and in return for that had impoverished his exchequer and shattered his health. He returned to Bordeaux a disappointed man. Don Pedro had failed in all his promises, and the only results of this expedition to the prince were broken health and crippled resources.

A change seems to have come over the prince's character after this. He lost his bright confidence and cheerful fearlessness, and became morose and discontented. He was pressed by the want of the necessary money to keep up the expenses of his extravagant court, and this and his illness weighed down his spirits. To his enemies, who had so long trembled before him, it seemed that the hour had come when they might safely attack him.

By the treaty of Bretigny, Edward III. had promised to renounce for ever his claim to the French crown; and in return, the French king had promised to renounce his sovereignty over the English provinces in France, which were henceforth to be held as independent possessions owing no right of allegiance to the French crown. Time had passed on, and for one reason or another the formal renunciation of these claims had never been made. It was perhaps only natural that both sides should put off as long as possible the moment when they must definitely give up what they had so long clung to.

Charles V., King of France, had probably never really intended to conform to the peace of Bretigny. It had been concluded in his father's lifetime, and had been wrung from him only by the miserable condition of France, after the Battle of Poitiers. For the moment he was ready to agree to anything, and wait for the time when he might be able to win back what he had lost. Part of the ransom of King John was still unpaid. With characteristic generosity, Edward had allowed many of the hostages to go to France, on giving their word that they would come back. But most of them never returned, and his demands to Charles for payment of the rest of the money passed unheeded.

Charles, who was quietly gathering strength whilst he waited a favourable moment for attacking the Black Prince, must have seen with delight the false step which his enemy took in aiding Pedro the Cruel. It soon became clear how fruitless the Spanish expedition had been. The prince had hardly reached Bordeaux, when Henry of Trastamare, who had been attacking the frontiers of Aquitaine, withdrew his army thence, and crossed the Pyrenees into Arragon, to prepare for a second invasion of Castile. He was anxious to have again the aid of Du Guesclin; but Du Guesclin unfortunately was still a prisoner in the Black Prince's hands, and knew not how to raise the money wanted for his ransom.

One day, when the prince was in good humour, he called Du Guesclin to him, and asked him how he was.

"I was never better, my lord," was the answer; "I cannot be otherwise than well, for I am, though in prison, the most honoured knight in the world."

"How so?" asked the prince.

"They say in France, as well as in other countries," answered Du Guesclin, "that you are so much afraid of me, and have such a dread of my gaining my liberty, that you dare not set me free; and this is my reason for thinking myself so much valued and honoured."

The prince did not like this, for he knew that it was partly the truth. He at once offered Du Guesclin his liberty, for a much smaller sum than had been asked before. His council tried to dissuade him from keeping this agreement; but the prince, speaking like a good and loyal knight, said, "Since we have granted it, we will keep it, and not act in any way contrary."

It was not long before Du Guesclin was able to pay the money, and hastened to join Henry, who was already successfully invading Castile. Most of the towns opened their gates to him, and he defeated Pedro in battle, and pursued him to the fortress of Montiel. Here, by some means or other, Pedro and Henry met face to face. So great was their hatred for one another, that Pedro immediately threw himself upon his brother, and being the stronger, threw him down upon the ground under himself; but Henry managed to draw his long Spanish knife, and plunging it into Pedro, killed him on the spot. After this he was secure in his possession of the throne of Castile, and had no longer to fear any rival.

This event of course entirely destroyed any hopes the Black Prince might still have of getting the money due from Pedro. He had not enough money himself to pay more than half of what was due to the Companies which had fought under his banner. They, on being disbanded, went off to ravage the French territory, which did not tend to make the French feel more friendly to the Black Prince's rule. In truth it is impossible to deny that he showed little talent as an administrator in his position as ruler of Aquitaine.

His subjects were rapidly growing more and more discontented, and many of the chief nobles, who had at first crowded to swear allegiance to him through mere terror of his name, now began secretly to draw near to France. By a fatal mistake of policy he managed to estrange his subjects still further. He was deeply in debt, and had no money either to defray the expenses of his court, or to prepare for a new struggle with France, which he felt must soon be inevitable. He felt, therefore, that it was necessary to impose a tax upon his subjects; and he hit upon the most burdensome tax he could have discovered. He proposed to the Assembly of the States of his duchy that a hearth tax should be levied for five years; that is, that for every fire upon the hearth an annual duty should be paid. This kind of tax was particularly oppressive, as it fell unequally; the poor pay more in proportion to their small means than do the rich. Hence the tax caused great discontent, especially amongst the Gascon barons, the lords of Armagnac, d'Albret, Cominges, and many others.

The whole duchy seemed to weary of the English rule. The people resented, naturally enough, the ravages and extortions of the Free Companies, and complained that the English nobles were arrogant and overbearing. The King of France watched eagerly this growing discontent; but He remained quiet until he had concluded an offensive and defensive alliance with Henry of Trastamare. The Gascon lords, in their discontent at the new tax, claimed to have a right of appeal to the King of France, as if he had still been the feudal superior of the duchy, to whom the vassals might carry their complaints against their lord.

This claim of appeal greatly angered the Black Prince; for in the treaty of Bretigny the King of France had agreed to renounce all rights over Aquitaine, and therefore could receive no appeals. But the Gascons said that it was not in the power of the King of France to renounce these rights without the consent of the barons and cities of Aquitaine; and this consent had never been given, and would never be given. The dispute, as was natural, only increased the ill-will between the prince and his subjects.

From all sides the King of France was advised to seize this favourable moment for attacking the prince. He was told that, as soon as he declared war, all the barons and cities of Aquitaine would turn to his side; for all were discontented with the English rule. At last, on the 25th January, 1369, he summoned the Black Prince to appear before the court of his peers at Paris, and answer the complaints brought against him by his vassals. This proceeding was, of course, entirely contrary to the treaty of Bretigny. It was treating the prince as if he were a vassal of France; whereas, according to the treaty, the King of France had entirely renounced his claim to the allegiance of Aquitaine. By treating the Black Prince as a vassal, he therefore distinctly threw down the gauntlet of war.

Great was the anger of the prince when this summons reached him. When the commissioners who had brought the letter had read it to him, he looked at them for a moment in silence, and then burst forth in rage.

"We will willingly come to Paris on the day appointed," he said; "but it will be with our helmet on our head, and sixty thousand men at our back."

He would give no other answer to the commissioners; and after they had gone, his anger burnt so hot against them that he sent some of his knights after them, to seize them and bring them back to prison.

"Let them not," he said, "go and tell their prattle to the Duke of Anjou, who loves us little, and say how they have summoned us personally in our own palace."

The King of France was indignant when he heard of the answer of the Black Prince, and of the treatment which his commissioners had met with. He made immediate preparations for war. He sent a challenge to the King of England by a common valet, a kitchen-boy, that he might make it as insulting as possible.

Both England and its king were sunk in the enjoyments of peace. The king was growing old, and loved ease and luxury. The country was weary of war, and absorbed in trade and manufacture. Still the challenge of the King of France stung their pride, and threw Edward III. into a mighty passion. He determined to reassert his claim to the crown of France, and opened the war with vigour. He sent the Duke of Lancaster with an army to Calais to invade the north of France, and his son Edmund, Duke of Cambridge, with troops to assist the Black Prince in Aquitaine. The Black Prince established his camp at Angoulême. The services of the various Free Companies were eagerly bid for by both the combatants, and many were engaged on either side.

The French soon began their inroads upon the prince's territory. He lay at Angoulême helpless from illness, and almost wild with vexation at hearing of the advances of his enemies. A desultory warfare began, in which neither side gained any considerable advantage; but the French seemed to be pressing on further, whilst the disaffection of the chief nobles and the illness of the prince tended more and more to break up the unity of the English provinces.

In the north the Duke of Lancaster did nothing but burn and ravage the enemy's country. The French Army, which had been sent against him, had been expressly ordered not to engage battle; the remembrance of the English victories was still too vivid in the minds of the French.

The death, in a chance skirmish, of his valued friend and wise counsellor, Sir John Chandos, was a serious blow to the prince. He was *seneschal* of Poitou, and was very anxious to drive back the French, who had taken some strong places there. He attacked a body of the enemy much superior in number to his own force, and fell upon them with scoffs and jeers. But as he was advancing on foot, he slipped on the ground, made slippery by the frost. He was entangled in the long robe of white samite, which he wore under his armour according to the fashion of those days, and stumbled. A French squire seized this opportunity to make a thrust at him; Sir John had lost an eye five years before, and the thrust being made on his blind side, he could not see to ward it off. To the dismay of his followers, he fell back rolling in death-agony on the ground. They fought desperately, eager to revenge his fall, but owing to their small number were obliged to surrender to the French.

Soon after they were released by the arrival of a large body of

English troops, to whom the French in their turn had to yield. Chandos was discovered lying so severely wounded that he was unable to speak. Great were the lamentations of the English; for all loved and revered him. There was no knight more valiant or courteous than he. His servants gently disarmed him, and he was laid on a litter made of shields and targets, and so was slowly carried at a foot-pace to Mortemer, the nearest fort. He only lived one day and night, and was buried by his friends at Mortemer. On his tomb was written this epitaph in French:

> I, *John Chandos, an English knight,*
> *Seneschal of all Poitou,*
> *Against the French king oft did fight,*
> *On foot and horseback many slew.*
> *Bertrand du Guesclin prisoner too*
> *By me was taken in a vale,*
> *At Lensac did the foe prevail;*
> *My body then at Mortemer*
> *In a fair tomb did my friends inter,*
> *In the year of grace divine,*
> *Thirteen hundred sixty-nine.*

Froissart says of Chandos, that never since a hundred years did there exist one more courteous, nor fuller of every virtue and good quality. What the English cause lost by his death can hardly be estimated. His valour and wisdom might have prevented the loss of Aquitaine.

It was early in 1370 that Chandos was slain. That year Charles V. determined to strike a decisive blow. Two armies, under his brothers the Dukes of Anjou and Berry, the former assisted by the great General Du Guesclin, were to invade Aquitaine at the same time. They advanced with great success, taking one city after another. Limoges, the capital of Limousin, was surrendered into their hands by its bishop, who turned traitor. News of the loss of this important city was brought to the Black Prince as he lay upon his bed of sickness. In a frenzy of rage he sat up in his bed, and exclaimed, "The French hold me dead; but if God give me relief, and I can once leave this bed, I will again make them feel."

Now that it was too late to gain the affections of his people, he had at the advice of Edward III. remitted the hearth tax; but this seemed to the people only a sign of weakness. He also offered in the name of his father the royal pardon to all those who had revolted, if they would return to their allegiance. The Duke of Lancaster had arrived in Aquitaine to aid him in the conduct of affairs, on account of his broken health. The Black Prince's authority in Aquitaine seemed to be gone; but the French successes, the loss of Limoges, and the treachery of its bishop, roused him to make a last effort. He swore by the soul of his father that he would have Limoges back again, and would make the inhabitants pay dearly for their treachery. He mustered his forces at Cognac, and prepared to march towards Limoges. When he took the field, and all his men-at-arms were drawn out in battle array, the whole country was filled with fear: his name had not yet lost its terror. He could not mount on horseback, but was obliged to be carried in a litter. He found Limoges well defended, but he made his army encamp all round it, and swore he would never leave the place till he had taken it.

Limoges was too well garrisoned to be taken by assault, and the English therefore prepared to lay siege to it. They had with them a large body of miners, and the prince gave orders that the walls should be mined. After a month all was ready. The garrison of the town tried by countermining to destroy the work of the prince's miners, but failed; and the miners having filled their mines with combustibles, set fire to them. The explosion threw down a large piece of the wall. The English, who were all ready and waiting for the right moment, rushed in through the breach, whilst others attacked the gates. So quickly was it done that the French had no time to resist. Then the prince, borne on his litter, and John of Gaunt, and the other nobles, rushed into the town with their men. The soldiers, eager for booty, ran through the town, killing men, women, and children, according to the orders given by the prince from his litter. Froissart says:

> It was a most melancholy business, for all ranks, ages, and sexes cast themselves on their knees before the prince, begging for mercy; but he was so inflamed with passion and revenge that he listened to none, but all were put to the sword wherever they could be found.

The garrison meanwhile had drawn themselves up in a body, and stood with their backs to an old wall, determined to fight to the last. The Duke of Lancaster and the Earl of Cambridge advanced to attack them, and in order to be on an equality with them, dismounted from their horses before they began the fight. The English were greatly superior in number; but the French fought so bravely that they were able to hold their own for some little time. The prince watched the combat with deep interest. The sight of the bravery of the knights at last roused again his nobler and more generous emotions, and he shouted out that the lives of those French knights who would surrender should be spared. Whereupon the French gave up their swords and yielded themselves prisoners. The bishop was also taken prisoner. The whole town was burnt and pillaged, and utterly destroyed. The Black Prince, worn out with suffering and disease, seemed to wish to revenge himself by one act of relentless cruelty for the loss of all his power and authority in France.

The sack of Limoges shows us the dark side of chivalry. We must not blame the Black Prince too severely for it. In sacrificing the innocent inhabitants of a whole city to his revenge, he was only acting in accordance with the spirit of the age in which he lived. The views of life in which he had been educated had taught him no respect for human life as such. His generous emotions were not called out by the piteous suffering of women and children, but by the brave fighting of men-at-arms. This was what chivalry led to, and all its bright features cannot make us forgive its disregard of human suffering.

Doubtless this terrible sack is a blot upon the Black Prince's character; but we could hardly have hoped to find him superior to his age. In this as much as in his nobler deeds he is a true type of chivalry, and shows us how very partial and one-sided was its civilizing effect. We must remember also, in his excuse, that he was at that time suffering from a severe and painful illness, and suffering even more bitterly in mind at the loss of his proud position, and the breakup of his dominions. But whilst trying to see what may be said in his excuse, we must not shut our eyes to the enormity of the crime. The massacre of this innocent population could do no good, and could have no beneficial result. What the Black Prince did was to sacrifice all the inhabitants of a prosperous city to his own thirst for revenge.

After the sack he returned to Cognac, where he had left the princess. There he disbanded his forces, feeling too ill for any further enterprise. This one exertion seems to have had a bad effect upon him; for he became rapidly worse, to the great alarm of all around him. His physicians ordered him to return at once to England, and in sadness of heart he prepared to leave his duchy.

Just before he left he had the misfortune also to lose his eldest son, the little Prince Edward. He left his authority in Aquitaine to his brother, John of Gaunt, and sailed from Bordeaux with his wife and his son Richard in the beginning of the year 1371.

The voyage was prosperous. He soon reached England, and went to Windsor to meet the king. He had left his country full of hope and confidence; he returned broken down in health and spirits. The tide of English prosperity had turned, and it is melancholy to compare the bright beginning of Edward III.'s power with the last sad years of his reign.

CHAPTER 15

English Politics

The England to which the Black Prince returned was in many ways different from the England which he had left. The country had suffered one great loss; the good Queen Philippa, so long the faithful wife of Edward III., had died in 1369. By her wisdom and virtue she had been of great use to the king, and had been beloved through all the kingdom. Deprived of her counsel, Edward fell under the influence of one of the ladies of her bedchamber, Alice Perrers, a woman of great wit and beauty, who ruled him at her will, and who was used as a tool by the different political parties.

It was a melancholy end for the bright, vigorous king to come to. The external splendour and glory of his reign was gone. His court had lost its brilliancy. He himself seemed almost to have sunk into a premature dotage. But though the last years of his reign were not as brilliant as the former years, they are perhaps more important for the history of our country; for in them we see the beginning of a great political struggle, which left most important traces upon the development of our constitution; and we are also able to trace the remarkable increase of the power and influence of Parliament. In these struggles the Black Prince, for the first time in his life, appeared as a politician; and the part which he took in them earned for him as much glory as his victories of Poitiers or Najarez.

All through Edward's reign Parliament had been increasing in power; but we shall not be able to understand the way in which it had developed, unless we go back and try to find out what it was at the beginning of Edward's reign.

There had always been under the Norman kings a Great Council, composed of the chief men of the kingdom, by whose assent and consent the Crown acted. But besides the advice of their nobles, the kings felt the need of the money of their people; and to obtain this the more easily, they summoned some of them to sit side by side with their advisers in the Great Council. The old arrangement of the shires and the shire courts gave a means of getting representatives. First, knights, to be chosen from every shire, were summoned to the meetings of the Great Council; and finally, Simon de Montfort, in 1264, summoned also burgesses from the chief cities.

Edward I.'s pressing need for money drove him to follow the example of Simon de Montfort, and summon these representatives to Parliament for the purpose of obtaining from them more easily grants of money.

This privilege, however, of sending representatives to Parliament was not one which the towns were eager to grasp. The burgesses did not care to leave their business, and undertake an expensive and dangerous journey to attend the Parliament. It was an arrangement more for the King's convenience than for theirs. When they got there they had nothing to do but vote grants of money. It was only slowly, and without any outward struggle, that the knights, who represented the shires, and the burgesses, who represented the cities, came to take any part in legislation. It was in this respect that the reign of Edward III. saw a great change.

In the Parliaments of Edward I. each order had deliberated separately. The clergy, the barons, the knights, and the burgesses made their grants separately. At first the barons and the knights, whose interests were very similar, tended to combine. The importance of the burgesses, however, increased during the reign of Edward II., as the barons needed their aid in the struggle against the Crown. As they increased in importance the knights of the shire seem to have broken off their connexion with the barons, and joined with the burgesses. We do not know how this change was brought about; but in the beginning of the reign of Edward III. we find the knights and burgesses combined together under the name of *the Commons*.

That the knights of the shire united with the burgesses, and not with the barons, is a fact of immense importance in our constitutional history. Had they united with the barons, the aristocratic party would have been the strongest in the State. As it was, the Commons, the people, were to be the strongest.

In the reign of Edward III., therefore, we find Parliament divided very much as it now is, into the Upper and Lower Houses. The clergy still sat apart, and formed what is now called the House of Convocation. Only the spiritual peers, that is, the members of the higher clergy, who by holding land directly from the Crown were in the same position as the barons, sat in the Upper House of Parliament.

It was during the reign of Edward III. that the Commons first began to feel their power and importance, and really to desire the privilege of sitting in Parliament. This is one of the signs of the progress they made at this time. They were eager to make laws, and the king himself shared their eagerness, and in consequence this reign is marked by fussy legislation on many different points.

Trade and manufactures were the great interests of the age, and they were represented by the men of the commons, whose minds were entirely occupied by such matters, and whose desire was to benefit them, as they thought, by making laws for their regulation. They had not learnt the great lesson, that trade prospers best when it is left alone by law-makers. They were inexperienced in making laws, and charmed with their new power, thought it would be easy to make the world go rightly by making laws about everything. Continually the laws when made were found to have quite different results to what the law-makers had expected, and had to be repealed the next year.

This restless desire to interfere in everything was very harmful to trade and industry. There were so many changes that people found it difficult to know what the law really was. Many of the laws were not attended to at all, as it was impossible to watch over the people narrowly enough to see that they were obeyed. We have seen how Parliament tried to fix the price of labour. In the same way it tried to fix the price of everything else. It fixed the price at which tailors should make clothes, at which poultry, meat, bread, and all other articles of ordinary consumption were to be sold. Even the number of dishes which a man might have for dinner was fixed by law.

These laws have left no permanent impression on English history, and are interesting only as giving indications of the manners and customs of the times. They serve also to show how greatly the energy of Parliament increased in this reign, even though it was misdirected. There are other and more important things which show us the great increase of its power.

It had always been the theory of the English Constitution, that the king could not raise money without the consent of the Great Council of the Realm; but this had often been little more than a theory. In this reign it became a clearly recognized fact, that no money could be raised except with the consent of Parliament, and we find Edward

III. always appealing to Parliament in his necessities. Parliament also established its right to petition against grievances, and so insisted upon the necessity of both Houses agreeing before any change could be made in the laws.

Edward III. held frequent Parliaments, and made it his practice to consult them on all matters, even on what had been always supposed to belong entirely to the king, the making of war and peace. He seemed to wish to throw upon Parliament the responsibility of his expensive wars. Probably he hoped that if the war was ostensibly carried on by the advice of Parliament, it would be easier to obtain grants of money for its expenses. The Commons, however, were not very eager to advise on these difficult points, saying that they were too simple and ignorant to be able to do so, and promising to agree to anything which the king and his council might decide upon.

In raising money for his wars, Edward III. drew largely from the clergy, whose wealth made them very tempting subjects for taxation. The clergy had long claimed immunity from taxation, and from all the burdens of the State, but in this age they could not hope to enforce such a claim. They were the wealthiest class in the land. When the French wars increased the necessities of the Crown, and obliged Edward to demand large subsidies from Parliament, all eyes were turned to the clergy as the body who, though not touched by the general taxes, was yet most able to contribute money. The clergy could not refuse the king's demands; but when they had to pay money to the king, they became more unwilling to send the Pope the subsidies which he demanded.

The Popes at this time were both poorer and more avaricious than they had been before. They regarded England as their great source of wealth, and demanded large sums of money from the clergy. The effect of this was to put the English clergy as a body in opposition to the Pope, and to make them more national in their feelings than they had been before. They placed the interests of their country far before the interests of the papacy.

This was a time of great degradation for the papacy, which had sunk so low as almost to lose men's reverence. The cause of this degradation lay in the struggle which had taken place sometime before between Philip the Fair, King of France, and Pope Boniface VIII. Boniface's ambition had led him to try and set up the power of the papacy over the affairs of every country of Europe. But Philip the Fair would not brook his interference in France. He quarrelled with him, and sent men to seize and ill-treat him in his own palace. Boniface died through rage and despair at this insult. Philip, after trying in vain to get complete submission out of the next Pope, at last succeeded in getting a Pope of his own choosing in Clement V. He promised obedience to Philip, and fixed his abode at Avignon instead of Rome, that he might be nearer the French king.

Avignon was in Provence, just outside the French border, in the dominions of the King of Naples. For seventy years the seat of the papacy remained there, and this has been called the time of the Babylonish captivity. The Popes during this period acted in the interests of the French king. Most of them were French by birth; all of them were French in their sympathies. Their European position seemed lost, and with it the awe and reverence with which they had been regarded. The English, at war with France, were not likely to bear the encroachments made by a French Pope, and clergy, laity, and king joined together to repel them.

The first great statute directed against the interference of the Pope was the Statute against Provisors, passed in 1351. The Pope was in the habit of making *provisions* for vacant benefices by appointing to them men of his own choice, and it was against this custom that the statute was directed. It naturally seemed very unjust to Englishmen, that English benefices should be given away to cardinals and other members of the Papal court, who drew the revenues from their benefices without ever coming near them; but we must remember that at this time great benefices were not bestowed upon men as rewards for spiritual eminence. They were the prizes which were given to great statesmen, to courtiers, and royal favourites.

The ecclesiastics appointed by the King of England had no more intention of residing on their benefices than the ecclesiastics appointed by the Pope. The Pope only claimed the right to reward his servants in the same way as the king did. This arrangement, by which Pope and king alike used the Church revenues for their own purposes, was too convenient for Edward III. to make him really eager for any reformation. The Statute of Provisors might forbid papal provisions, but it was never strictly kept; nor did the Statute which followed it, called from its first word in the original Latin, the Statute of Præmunire, prove more successful.

This statute forbade any appeals being made from the king's courts to the papal court, and forbade the introduction of papal bulls into England without royal permission.

The great interest of these statutes lies in the fact that they express the growing hostility aroused in the laity by the ambition and wealth of the clergy. The writings of the times are filled with complaints of the abuses among the clergy. Langland tells us in a fine passage in the *Vision of Piers Plowman* the miserable pass that religion had come to in those days—

And now is religion a rider, a roamer by streets;
A leader of love-days, and a land-buyer;
A pricker on a palfrey from manor to manor;
An heap of houndes at his ears, as he a lord were,
And but if his knave knele that shal his cap bringe,
He loureth[1] on him, and asketh him who taught him courtesy.

The whole poem is full of allusions to the manner of life of the clergy, their ill-gotten wealth, and the neglect of their duties. In another place he says—

That have cure under Christ, and crowning[2] in token
And signe that they should shrive their parishioners,
Preach and pray for them and the poor faith,
Live in London in Lent and other times;
Some serve the Kinge, and his silver tellen
In chequer and in chancery.

In an extravagant age the clergy were especially marked by their wild and foolish extravagance, their love for fine clothes, for the chase, for show and pageantry of all kinds. Even the mendicant orders partook of this, and the Franciscan Friars, who had pledged themselves to the most absolute poverty, amassed wealth, and only obeyed the dictates of their order by abstaining from all labour. As a political ballad of the time says—

Full wisely do they preche and say,
But as they preche nothing do they.
And even of their preaching Langland says—
I find these friars, all the four orders,
Preach to the people for profit of themselven,
Glosed the gospel as them good liked.

The Church seemed to have lost all its early simplicity, and to have

---
1. Scowls.
2. The tonsure or shaven crown on the priest's head.

departed entirely from the teaching of the apostles.

The clergy absorbed all the chief offices of state. This had come about naturally, from the fact that till now they had been the only educated body in the state, and so they only had been fit to transact its business. But now learning had become more general. A new class, that of the lawyers, was springing up, and men were no longer willing to see everything in the hands of the clergy. The great opponent of their power was John of Gaunt, Duke of Lancaster, the king's third son. He was an ambitious and unscrupulous man, and his aim was to get the entire control of affairs during the last years of Edward III.'s reign. His opposition to the clergy sprung only from his own personal ambition; he wished to exclude the clergy from the offices of the state that he might fill them with his own creatures. The power of the Commons was as hateful in his eyes as the power of the clergy. He put himself at the head of a reactionary body of great barons, who wished to bring back the old order of things, and restore the power of their own order.

With John of Gaunt was united a man of a very different stamp. This was John Wiclif, who by his learning had risen into importance in the University of Oxford. He had shown himself an eager student, well versed in logic and metaphysics, deeply learned in theology, and delighting in the mathematical and natural sciences. The university had not been slow to recognise his distinction. He had been made fellow of Merton, then the leading college; afterwards he was master of Balliol Hall; and lastly, he had been made warden of Canterbury Hall, the new college founded by Simon Islip, Archbishop of Canterbury. He was first called into political prominence in 1366, when Edward III. called upon him to answer the demand made by Pope Urban VI. for the homage of England, and the tribute promised by King John. In his answer, whilst calling himself the humble and obedient son of the Roman Church, he clearly showed how determined he was to take the national side, and resist papal encroachments. He was equally opposed to the ambition and wealth of the clergy, and this was the cause of his connexion with John of Gaunt.

It is impossible to believe that there can have been any real sympathy between the two men,—Wiclif, the zealous student and austere reformer; and John of Gaunt, the complete man of the world, corrupt in his life, narrow and unscrupulous in his policy, absorbed in selfish ambition. They had, however, this in common—that each wished to destroy the power of the clergy, though from very different motives.

John of Gaunt wished to humiliate the Church; Wiclif wished to purify it. John of Gaunt resented the official arrogance of the bishops, and their large share of temporal power; Wiclif hoped to restore the long lost apostolical purity of the Church.

It was in the Parliament of 1371 that the first great blow at the power of the clergy was struck. The Duke of Lancaster was away in Aquitaine; but we cannot doubt that Parliament was inspired by his influence, when it petitioned the king that only secular men might be employed in his court and household. Chief amongst the clergy in high office at that time was William of Wykeham, Bishop of Winchester, the Lord High Chancellor.

He had first become important as the king's surveyor and architect at Windsor. Here the king had undertaken important and extensive works for the improvement and extension of the castle. Wykeham had a strong natural taste for architecture, and seems moreover to have been a wise and practical man of business. He became the king's chaplain, his principal secretary, and the keeper of the Privy Seal. In 1367 he was elevated to the see of Winchester, and appointed Lord Chancellor.

He was a most liberal man, and had the interests of the people sincerely at heart. To posterity he is chiefly known by his munificence in founding Winchester School, and New College at Oxford, two foundations which have greatly promoted the cause of learning. He seems in all cases to have used his power and his wealth for the public good. But John of Gaunt and his party hated him on account of his wealth and position; whilst in Wiclif's eyes he was not spiritual enough for a bishop. Wiclif thought that no ecclesiastic ought to hold office, or busy himself in secular affairs. He no doubt alludes to Wykeham when he says bitterly:

Benefices, instead of being bestowed on poor clerks, are heaped .... on one wise in building castles, or in worldly business.

It was against Wykeham that the petition of Parliament against giving office to ecclesiastics was chiefly directed. He was forced to resign the seals. The other ecclesiastics in office had to give up their posts, and laymen, creatures of John of Gaunt, were appointed to fill them. Sir Richard le Scrope was appointed Treasurer, and Sir Robert Thorpe Lord Chancellor. The same Parliament also petitioned the King about the unsatisfactory state of the navy, and granted a subsidy for putting it into a proper condition; but no great expedition was planned to reconquer the lost possessions in France. The war went on in a desultory way, and nothing particular was gained on either side. The Commons were growing tired of paying for it. They further showed their animosity to the clergy by decreeing that the tax which was to be levied to provide the subsidy voted for the king, was to be raised also from all those lands which had passed into the hands of the clergy before the twentieth year of Edward I.

The clergy met together in Convocation in 1373 to consider what course they should take under these circumstances. They met in St. Paul's, where Whittlesey, Archbishop of Canterbury, presided. He was too weak, both in body and mind, to take an important part in the proceedings. He summoned all his strength to preach the opening sermon, after which he sunk down exhausted. Simon Sudbury, Bishop of London, a man of the Duke of Lancaster's party, succeeded him as president of Convocation. The conduct of the clergy was marked by moderation. They had no wish to resist obstinately the demands of the Commons; but they complained that they already had to tax themselves heavily to provide subsidies for the king, and to meet the demands of the Pope. They said that they would willingly give more to the king, if he would free them from the exactions of the Pope. The king caused an embassy to be sent to the Pope, stating the grievances of the clergy; but the Pope would do nothing but promise to send ambassadors to a congress to be held at some future time.

The Duke of Lancaster's party was now in complete possession of all power in the kingdom. It remained to be seen how far they would be able to win the confidence of the people. In the conduct of the war they had been by no means successful. The duke himself had not mended matters by marrying Constance, daughter of Pedro the Cruel, and assuming in her right the title of King of Castile. This only threw Henry of Trastamare more than ever on the side of France. In 1372 the Earl of Pembroke was sent with an English fleet to assist the Duke of Lancaster. But now the folly of having turned Spain into a bitter enemy became apparent. The English fleet was intercepted by a Spanish fleet, and completely defeated. Pembroke himself was taken prisoner, and the English naval power received a blow from which it took long to recover.

Disaster followed disaster in Aquitaine. Rochelle was seized by the French. Thouars, one of the last places of importance remaining to the English, was besieged and hard pressed. When news of all these misfortunes reached Edward III. he was roused from his lethargy, and determined to make one last effort to recover what he had lost. A fleet was equipped, in which Edward himself, and even the Black Prince, whose health was now somewhat better, embarked. But the fleet never reached France. It was beaten about by contrary winds for some weeks, and at last was obliged to return to England. There was now nothing to be done except to ask for a truce. In 1374 the Duke of Lancaster returned to England, leaving all the English possessions, except Bordeaux and Bayonne, in the hands of the French.

It was determined that a general congress should be held at Bruges to discuss terms of peace with France. To this congress the Pope and Edward III. were also to send commissioners, to discuss the points at issue between England and the Papacy.

John of Gaunt was chief amongst the English ambassadors, who went to Bruges to try and arrange a peace. John Wiclif went as one of the ecclesiastical commissioners, of whom the Bishop of Bangor was head. There were great difficulties in the way of any peace between England and France. The French wished Edward to give up Calais, but the English would not hear of this. It was only the earnest endeavours of the Pope, Gregory XI., a sincere lover of peace, which finally brought about a truce, to last till June, 1376.

Meanwhile the ecclesiastical commissioners were also very busy, and all waited eagerly to see the result of this conference. If Wiclif had allowed himself to hope that it would lead to any reform in the Church, he must have been bitterly disappointed. We do not know what part he took in it, but he must have soon seen with disgust that his fellow-commissioners had no desire for reform, and that the king himself was not more zealous than they. In September six lengthy bulls arrived in England from the Pope, stating the conclusions arrived at by the conference. These bulls showed that nothing really had been agreed upon. The Pope made no promises for the future, but only arranged some informalities in the past. It seemed as if the king and the Pope had come to an agreement, purely for their own personal advantage. Each was really to do pretty much as he liked, and the great questions which involved the interests of the Church and the nation were left untouched.

CHAPTER 16

The Good Parliament

Whatever men might have hoped from the Congress at Bruges, and from the lay ministry formed by the influence of John of Gaunt and his party, all their hopes were now disappointed. They had hoped for reform in the Church, and all they obtained was a compact with the papacy for the maintenance of old abuses. The man who had been foremost in making this compact, the Bishop of Bangor, was rewarded by translation by papal provision to the see of Hereford. This was what the lay ministry had done for the Church after all its promises of reform. And what had become of the money which they had voted for the continuance of the war? How had the war been conducted? A few short years before France had lain crushed and humbled at the feet of England; now nothing remained of all that the Black Prince had won in France, except Bayonne, Bordeaux, Calais, and a few other unimportant places. The English navy had been annihilated; the English coasts had been insulted by the enemy; never had England known such degradation.

Men had believed in the Duke of Lancaster, and this was what he had led them to. Now men saw his personal aims, his selfish ambition. All the tide of popular fury was turned against him and his ministers. He was accused, whether justly or not we cannot say, of designs on the throne; since he knew that his brother, the Black Prince, could not live long. When he was dead nothing would stand between Lancaster and the throne but the young Prince Richard. There was no man more unpopular than he in England; for he was regarded as the opponent of the people's hero, the Prince of Wales.

But the people alone could do nothing against the power and influence of the duke. In their hour of need, however, they found a leader in the man who had so often led their armies victoriously against the enemy, in the Black Prince himself.

Parliament met at Westminster in the spring of 1376. It was three years since it had last met—an unusually long interval, considering the frequent Parliaments held in this reign. The Black Prince had moved to the royal palace at Westminster, that he might be able to watch over the proceedings. The king opened Parliament on the 28th of April; and on the following day the Lord Chancellor Knyvet addressed the Lords and the Commons assembled in the great chamber at Westminster. He told them briefly the reasons for which they had been summoned:

> First, to advise on the good government and peace of the kingdom of England; secondly, to consider for the external defence of the kingdom, by land as well as by sea; and thirdly, to make arrangements for the continuation of the war with France.

The Commons were then bidden to retire, and deliberate apart in their own chamber in the Chapter-house of the Abbey of Westminster. At the demand of the Commons, certain bishops and barons were appointed to deliberate with them, and give them their advice on the subject of the subsidy to be granted to the king. The next point was the choice of a Speaker, and the election made by the Commons was in itself a mark of their opposition to the Duke of Lancaster. Peter de la Mare, the man chosen, was the steward of Edmund Mortimer, Earl of March, who had married Philippa, the only child of Lionel Duke of Clarence, Lancaster's elder brother. Philippa had a prior right to the throne to that of John of Gaunt, and therefore she and her husband necessarily opposed his ambitious schemes. Peter de la Mare's policy was sure to be opposition to the duke. He was, a contemporary chronicler tells us:

> A man of abundant wisdom and courage; a lover of justice and truth; neither the bribes nor the threats of his enemies could deter him from the right course.

With regard to the demand for a subsidy, the Commons consented to grant the same sum as they had given three years before; more they would not give on account of the great scarcity throughout the land produced by the plague, the murrain amongst the cattle, and the failure of the crops. This matter once settled, the Commons proceeded to what they considered the chief business of the session, the petitions about grievances. Headed by Peter de la Mare, they carried their answer about the subsidy to the council and the barons.

Then, standing before the nobles, amongst whom John of Gaunt stood foremost, the speaker began to disclose the grievances of the country. The people, he complained, were exceedingly weighed down by taxes; but even this they would have borne patiently had the money been usefully employed; yet in spite of the great expenditure the wars had not prospered. The Commons demanded an account of the way in which the money had been spent. The speaker concluded:

Neither is it credible that the king should want such an infinite treasure, if they were faithful that served him.

Great was the indignation of Lancaster at this insolence of the Commons, as he called it. Full of wrath, he declared his intention of silencing them next day by a show of his power; but his followers pointed out to him that the Commons had the support of the Black Prince, his brother, and that he could not crush them. Afraid lest they should go further, and allow disclosures to be made about the evil manner of his own life, he appeared before them next day seemingly mild and gracious. Then the Commons went on with their proceedings. They stated that, on account of the great wars abroad, the present council was insufficient to manage the affairs of the state; and they asked that ten or twelve bishops, lords, and others be added to strengthen the council. They next unfolded a long list of grievances, which showed the disordered condition and the maladministration of the country.

They petitioned, first of all, that the king's guilty officers be punished, they insisted that such heavy taxation would not have been necessary, considering the immense amount of money that had come into the kingdom as ransoms for French prisoners, if only it had been properly and honestly administered. They promised that the king should have no difficulty in getting plenty of money for the war, and his other necessities, if he would first dismiss and punish his ministers. They attacked Richard Lyons, a London merchant, and a creature of the duke's. He had had patents granted him by members of the council, to buy up merchandise, and sell it again at his own price; he had also caused customs to be put upon wool and other commodities, which he levied principally for his own profit.

It was no wonder that the duke, who interfered in this way with the trade of London, should draw upon himself the hatred of the Londoners. Lyons tried to save himself by sending a bribe to the Prince of

Wales, in the shape of a barrel containing £1,000. The prince refused it with scorn; but afterwards regretted his refusal, saying that he would have "done a good deed by sending it to the knights that travail for the realm." Lyons then sent his money to the king, who kept it, saying "that he took the same in part payment of the money that was owing to him; for this and much more he owed him, and had not presented him with anything but his own."

Lyons could not save himself. He was ordered to be imprisoned at the king's pleasure, to lose the freedom of the city, and have all his goods seized.

Next followed the impeachment of Lord Latimer, another creature of the duke's, who was Chamberlain and Privy Councillor, and governor of a castle in Brittany, where he had appropriated large sums of money, and had taken bribes to surrender places to the French. He was also sentenced to be fined and imprisoned. Other accusations followed, all founded on much the same charge—appropriation of the public money. One man, William Ellis, an accomplice of Lyons, had extorted money at Yarmouth from ships driven by stress of weather into the port. Another, John Peachy, had obtained from Lyons a patent giving him the exclusive right of selling sweet wines in London. Sir John Neville was sentenced to be fined and imprisoned, because he had allowed some soldiers whom he was conducting to France to ravage the country all the way to Southampton.

The Commons declared in plain terms that the people of England would no longer consent to have their interests trampled upon, and their trade interfered with, for the sake of enriching a greedy baronage and its creatures. In all this they were firmly supported and encouraged by the Prince of Wales and the good Bishop William of Wykeham, who was quite restored to the favour of the people. In fact, the Black Prince had seen that the best policy would be to attempt to unite against the baronage the Commons and the national clergy. The Commons were quite ready to welcome the clergy back to office; for they now saw only too well the selfish policy which had made John of Gaunt wish to drive them out.

But the Commons did not stop short with attacking the evil counsellors of John of Gaunt; they went on to impeach Alice Perrers, the woman who had gained such an unworthy influence over the king in his old age. They passed an ordinance against:

Certain women of the court, and especially Alice Perrers, who interfered with the course of justice in the kingdom, sitting side by side on the bench with the judges.

Alice Perrers was examined before the nobles, and banished from the court. She was obliged to swear that she would keep away from the king.

It was by its vigorous attack upon all these abuses, and its desire to restore an orderly and discreet administration, that this Parliament earned for itself the name of "The Good Parliament." It established the right of Parliament to demand the redress of grievances, and to impeach the king's ministers. When we remember that at the beginning of the reign of Edward III. the one function of the Commons was to vote subsidies, we shall realize how great the increase of the power and influence of Parliament must have been during the reign, to admit of such proceedings as those of the Good Parliament taking place. Parliament was now strong enough to cause the ministers of the crown to be removed, and new ones more pleasing to it to take their place. Knyvet, the Lord Chancellor, was the only one of the old ministry who was retained.

CHAPTER 17

Death of the Black Prince

For the moment the people's cause had triumphed in Parliament. Meanwhile the people's friend was slowly passing away.

The Black Prince had been afflicted for five years with a grievous malady; but he had never been heard to murmur against the will of God. His sufferings had been very great; he was often so ill that his servant took him for dead. He had rallied his last strength that he might give Parliament his support in its struggle against the Duke of Lancaster. For this purpose he had, as we have seen, moved to the royal palace of Westminster. There he lay in his father's great chamber, and felt that his end was drawing very near.

Two contemporary chroniclers have given us an account of his death, so that we are able to form a tolerably accurate picture of the scene around his death-bed.

He bade them open the door of his room, that all his followers might come in. When all those who had served him were gathered round his bed, he said to them, "Sirs, pardon me that I cannot give you, who have so loyally served me, a reward fitting your services; but God and His saints will render it to you." They all wept bitterly; for every one of them loved him tenderly. Then he gave them all rich gifts, and prayed the king that he would ratify these gifts; and calling his little son to his bedside, he bade him never change or take away the gifts which he had given to his servants. Then turning again to the earls and barons, and all his other followers who stood around his bedside, he said to them in a clear voice, "I commend to you my son, who is yet but young and small, and pray that as you have served me, so from your heart you would serve him."

He called also his father, and his brother the Duke of Lancaster, and commended to them his wife and his son. All promised him truly that they would comfort his son, and maintain him in his right.

Soon his sufferings became too great for him to see any one; and it was forbidden that any more should enter the room, where he lay prostrate in the pangs of death. One man, Richard Stury, a political opponent of the prince's, is said to have forced his way in; for what end we can hardly tell; perhaps to ask his forgiveness. But the prince roused himself in the midst of his sufferings to upbraid him, saying, "Now you see what you have long desired; but I pray God that He will make an end of your evil deeds." After this outburst, the prince sank back half fainting. Then the Bishop of Bangor approached, and bade him forgive all those who had offended him, and ask God for forgiveness of his own sins, praying also all those whom he had offended for forgiveness; but the only answer he could get from the prince was, "I will."

The good old bishop thought there must be some evil spirits present, who prevented him saying more, and so he began sprinkling the four corners of the room with holy water. Suddenly the prince lifted up his eyes to heaven, and said:

> God, I give Thee thanks for all Thy benefits. In all my prayers I beg Thy pity, and that Thou wouldest grant me pardon for those sins which against Thee I have wickedly wrought. Moreover also, from all men whom knowingly or unknowingly I have offended, I beg with my whole heart the favour of forgiveness.

With these words he fell back and died; and with him, says the chronicler, all hope of Englishmen departed.

Bitter was the lamentation for his death. An old chronicler who lived in the prince's days says:

> Him being present, they feared not the incursions of any enemies, nor the forcible meeting in battle. . . . Truly unless God holde under His blessed hand that the miserable Englishman be not trodden down, it is to be feared that our enemies, who compass us on every side, will rage upon us, even unto our utter destruction, and will take our place and country. Arise, Lord! help us and defend us for Thy name's sake.

Only the day before his death the prince had signed his will. In it he appointed William of Wykeham one of his executors, which shows us what confidence he placed in the bishop. His will contains the most minute directions as to his funeral. It was his express desire that he should be buried in the great cathedral of Canterbury, near the famous English saint, Thomas of Canterbury.

His body was therefore carried from the palace at Westminster, where he died, to Canterbury. There, as it entered the gates, it was met by a warrior, mounted on a prancing steed. He was armed for war, and bore the prince's arms quartered. Then came four men carrying banners, each of whom wore on his head a cap with the prince's arms. A few steps further on the funeral procession was met by a second knight. He also rode a stately steed; but he was armed for peace, and bore the prince's badge of ostrich feathers. Preceded by these warriors, the funeral procession advanced through the city till it reached the cathedral. Then the body of the brave prince was laid before the high altar, and vigils and masses were said in honour of it till the time came when it must be carried to its last resting-place in the Lady Chapel. There it was buried at a distance of ten feet from the shrine of the martyr St. Thomas, whom the prince, when alive, had always delighted to honour. Over it soon rose the noble monument which still marks the spot where lie the remains of the great warrior. Respecting his tomb also he had left minute directions.

The tomb was of marble, sculptured all round with twelve shields, each a foot high. On six of the shields were his arms, and on the other six his badge of ostrich feathers. On the top lay his recumbent figure, worked in relief in copper gilt. He was represented in full armour, wearing his helmet with his crest of a leopard engraved upon it. He himself composed the epitaph which is graven on his tomb; and it gives us a faithful picture of the mind of the man who wrote it.

It was written in French, and may be thus translated:

All ye that pass with closed mouth
By where this body reposes,
Hear this that I shall tell you,
Just as I know to say it.
Such as thou art, such was I:
You shall be such as I am;
Of death I never thought,
So long as I had life.
On earth I had great riches,
Of which I made great nobleness,
Land, houses, and great wealth,
Clothes, horses, silver, and gold:

But now I am poor and wretched;
Deep in the earth I lie;
My great beauty is all gone;
My flesh is all wasted;
Right narrow is my house;
With me nought but truth remains.
And if now ye should see me,
I do not think that you would say
That ever I had been a man,
So totally am I changed.
For God's sake pray the heavenly King
That He have mercy on my soul.
All they who pray for me,
Or make accord to God for me,
God give them His paradise,
Where no men are wretched.

We need find no difficulty in reading aright the character of the Black Prince. There are no contradictions to be accounted for; all is plain and straightforward. He was a simple God-fearing man, who did his duty, and led a life in accordance with the highest ideal of his times. He was not in advance of his day. We owe no great reforms, no marked steps in our national progress, to him. But he is the type of the noblest spirit of his times; he shows us the stuff of which Englishmen were made in those days. Friend and foe alike counted him the bravest warrior of that age. In battle he knew no fear, and had that kind of courage and energy which inspired the meanest man in his ranks to fight boldly like his prince. He was not only brave, but was a skilful general, and knew how to dispose his troops to the best advantage. In each of his three great victories he fought against fearful odds; and his success was due quite as much to the skilful grouping of his troops as to his bravery.

In the treatment of his prisoners he shows the beautiful courtesy of a true knight. Though we must blame him severely for his cruelty in the massacre of Limoges, we must remember that he only showed himself to be on a level with the morality of his day; moreover, he was aggravated by ill-health and suffering, and by the treachery of his subjects. In private life he seems to have shown great kindliness and consideration for others. He was beloved by all who came in contact with him. The noblest of English knights, Chandos, Felton, and many others, accompanied him on all his campaigns, and clung to him with a devotion which only personal love can have prompted. He forgot none of his servants, either on his death-bed or in his will. When in his last days he saw that the English people were suffering from misgovernment, and from the tyranny of his brother, moved with noble pity, he gathered his last strength that he might show himself their friend, and save them from oppression.

As far as we can judge from the scanty records of the chroniclers, he seems to have been much beloved by his wife, the fair maid of Kent, and to have lived with her in great happiness. He was a sincerely religious man; his special devotion to the Holy Trinity is repeatedly mentioned by the chroniclers, and we have seen how he never engaged in battle without earnest prayer. His good qualities are throughout those of a simple warrior. He had the genius of a soldier, not the genius of a ruler. When he first became ruler of Aquitaine, he seemed to be all-powerful. His name inspired such fear that no one would have ventured to attack him. It seemed an easy task to attach his subjects to himself, and form a well-consolidated principality which might safely resist the attacks of his enemies. But he lacked the qualities which would have enabled him to do this. He was no politician. He did not understand how to govern with economy, and develop his resources. Before a wise and crafty man like Charles V. of France he was powerless. He engaged in the fatal Spanish expedition, which ruined his health and drained his coffers. His dominions crumbled away; they were lost one by one without any battles, whilst he looked on helplessly at the ruin.

In reality his great victories were fruitless, and the wonderful success of the first half of Edward III.'s reign brought no lasting result. Edward III. was no more of a politician than his son. Instead of being content with what he had won, and making it secure, he indulged in wild schemes of ambition; and whilst dreaming about the French crown, he lost the Duchy of Aquitaine. It seems impossible to doubt that if Edward III. and his son had set about it in the right way, they might have secured for themselves the possession of Aquitaine. As it was, they not only lost what they had gained, but with it also what had come down to them from their fathers.

Yet we need not deplore this. For the progress of England it was far better that she should not be hampered with external possessions. The most important thing was, that England herself should grow strong before she thought of extending her dominions. Edward III.'s wars were useful to the progress of England, not because of the glory which they shed round his name, but because the great outlay which they involved drove him to call frequent Parliaments that he might raise supplies.

Thus a marked increase in the power and importance of Parliament is the only beneficial result of this war. In the main its results were most disastrous, and no wise and far-sighted ruler would ever have engaged in it. It caused the best energies of the country to be devoted to the pursuit of a chimerical object—the crown of France. For this object the resources of the country were drained, and the interests of the people were disregarded; whilst heavy taxes were laid upon them, which crippled their commerce and their industries. The bright promise of the opening of Edward III.'s reign found no fulfilment in the end. The chief legacy he left to his successors was enmity with France, and a restless desire to win back what he had lost. So whilst we admire the valour and energy of the Black Prince in the conduct of the wars, we cannot praise his father's wisdom in engaging in them. But we must remember that though in wisdom he was not before his age, in valour he surpassed his countrymen of all ages.

Chapter 18

The First Years of Richard II.

It is not possible to make a pause in the history of the times with the Black Prince's death. It will be well for us briefly to consider the events which followed it.

His death interrupted the reform begun by the Good Parliament by depriving it of his support, and prepared the way for his brother's return to power. John of Gaunt interfered in the most unscrupulous manner in the elections for the next Parliament, and so obtained the return of men who reversed the acts of the Good Parliament. William of Wykeham was again dismissed from office, and the nobles were once more triumphant. Alice Perrers was allowed to return to the old king, who lived at Eltham, alone and neglected. When he died, in 1377, at the age of sixty-five, even Alice Perrers deserted him after she had stolen the rings from his fingers. Richard II.'s accession was welcomed with joy by the Londoners, and a magnificent ceremony graced his coronation. As he was only in his twelfth year, a council of twelve was appointed to govern during his minority.

Meanwhile the attack of the nobles upon the Church went on, and Wiclif, in his zeal for reform, was working side by side with John of Gaunt. He was beginning to be regarded with suspicion and animosity by the Pope, and in 1377 was summoned to appear before Bishop Courtenay, of London, to answer the charges of heresy made against him. John of Gaunt was present to defend him, and spoke such insulting words to Courtenay that the Londoners, who loved their bishop, rushed to his rescue. They showed their hatred of Lancaster by sacking his palace of the Savoy; but they only objected to Wiclif in so far as he was Lancaster's friend. In his desires for reform they cordially sympathised; and when at the end of the same year he was again summoned to appear before the Archbishop at Lambeth, the Londoners broke in and dissolved the sittings of the court. Wiclif also found a friend in the Princess of Wales, the fair maid of Kent, who wrote to the bishop, telling him to desist from the proceedings against him. In the University of Oxford he was allowed to teach and lecture as he liked, and his schemes for Church reform were listened to with approval on all sides.

From his living of Lutterworth he sent forth itinerant preachers, who went, as the disciples of St. Francis had done before, to labour among the poor and the neglected. One of his great desires was to reform preaching, and these men were taught to preach the word of God in simplicity and purity, "where, when and to whom they could." They were called "the Simple Priests," and spoke to the people in simple homely language, spreading Wiclif's doctrines far and wide. For them Wiclif wrote many small tracts, which he published in large numbers, and in which he appealed to the people in their own language, and from their own point of view. He had set on foot a great spiritual revival, and if he had stopped short in his reforming tendencies, and had not gone on to deny the doctrine of transubstantiation, he might have come down to us canonised as St. John de Wiclif, the founder of a new order of preaching friars. But hopes of reform in the English Church were destined to be crushed for a time.

Wiclif published in Oxford twelve theses on the subject of transubstantiation. The chancellor felt himself bound to interfere, and forbid heretical teaching in the university. Wiclif appealed to the king to have the question settled.

At this moment all England was disturbed by the outbreak of the Peasants' Revolt. We have seen in speaking of the Black Death many of the causes of discontent amongst the peasantry. The wages of the labourers were fixed by law. Rigorous attempts were made to bind the peasant to the soil, and to restore the old conditions of serfdom. But since the days of serfdom there had been a great advance in the intelligence of the peasantry, who eagerly listened to the new views which the wandering preachers sent out by Wiclif were spreading over the country. It was said that all men were equal, and had equal rights. The popular rhyme:

When Adam delved and Eve span,
Where was then the gentleman?

ran from mouth to mouth. The iniquity of serfdom was becoming more and more clearly seen, and at the same time its oppressive character was making itself more and more harshly felt. The men who had served with courage and distinction in the French wars could not be expected to submit to their former serfage. A simultaneous rising of the peasantry in different parts of the country shows that the revolt had been long planned and carefully arranged. It was the result not of any one special act of tyranny, but of a long course of oppression, and above all of the attempt to return to the old system of exacting personal labour as payment for rent, instead of a money commutation.

The insurgents of Essex, under a leader who went by the name of Jack Straw, joined with the insurgents of Kent, under Wat the Tyler, and marched on London, striking terror by the way. The young king took refuge in the Tower. The insurgents entered London, and began their work of destruction. Their rage was especially directed against the lawyers. They destroyed the temple, with all its books and records. The foreign merchants in the city were also treated with great cruelty. Then the insurgents swarmed round the Tower, and demanded that the king should come out and hear their grievances. Richard II. was only a boy; but he knew no fear. Accompanied only by one or two attendants, he rode to Mile End, and listened to the grievances of the peasantry. He granted all they asked, and promised a general pardon to all concerned in the revolt.

But whilst this conference was going on, the remainder of the rebels had broken into the Tower, seized the Archbishop Simon Sudbury, and murdered him on Tower Hill. Their fury was directed against him, not as archbishop, but as chancellor. After this it was hardly to be hoped that there could be a peaceful end to the revolt. The next day, when quite by chance Richard met Wat the Tyler and his followers face to face, the peasant leader spoke so insolently that the Lord Mayor, Sir Richard Walworth, struck him to the ground with his dagger; and when the insurgents cried, "Kill, kill! they have killed our captain," Richard rode boldly to the front, saying, "What need ye, my masters? I am your captain and your king." The peasantry were easily touched. They gathered round Richard, kneeling, and asking his pardon.

The panic caused by the revolt was over. For a week the insurgents had kept the country in terror. Now Richard made a progress through the counties with forty thousand men at his back, and the rebels suffered stern and terrible justice for their revolt. The charters granted to the peasantry in the first moment of terror were revoked, and they seemed to have gained nothing by their rising. But they had shown the landholders their strength; and though no immediate change was made, it became more and more clear that the old conditions of serfdom could not be enforced.

It is quite certain that Wiclif had nothing to do with the rising of the peasants. Still, at the time it caused him and his teaching to be regarded with terror by the respectable classes of society. The communistic and socialistic views which had been spread among the people had in many cases been preached by men, who declared themselves followers of Wiclif. People were inclined to look upon the revolt as partly the outcome of his teaching, and so were no longer as ready as before to listen to his schemes for reform. Still Wiclif was not proceeded against with severity. Certain of his opinions were laid before a council of bishops and doctors of theology held in London, and were pronounced erroneous; but Wiclif himself was left in peace.

He stayed within the Church, living quietly in his vicarage of Lutterworth, and busying himself with his translation of the Bible till he died, on the 31st December, 1384. This translation of the Bible was the natural outcome of Wiclif's teaching. He had always insisted upon the necessity of the word of God being preached to everyone, and had said that the Scriptures were the common property of all men. But as long as the Bible existed only in the Latin tongue, it was a sealed book to the great majority of men. Wiclif's earnest belief that all men should know and study it for themselves led him to conceive the idea of translating it.

It was a great undertaking for one man to contemplate, and singlehanded he could never have accomplished it. He himself began with the New Testament whilst Nicholas of Hereford took the Old Testament in hand. This man was a doctor of theology, and one of the chief leaders of Wiclif's party in Oxford. He got as far in his translation as the book of Baruch, when he seems to have been suddenly interrupted, probably by proceedings conducted against him on account of his opinions.

Wiclif himself translated the entire New Testament, and probably finished the translation of the Old Testament. The next step was to get copies of the translation made, that it might be distributed amongst the people. This was done rapidly, and in 1382 copies of the separate books and portions were circulated widely.

This English translation was made from the Vulgate—that is, the Latin translation—and not from the original Greek or Hebrew. Nicholas of Hereford stuck very closely to the Latin forms, and was almost pedantically literal; so that he was hardly successful in making his translation readable. Wiclif's translation is very different. He wished above all to put into his work the spirit of the English language; to write in such a way that he might strike home to the hearts of his readers. Of all his English writings, his translation of the Bible is the most remarkable for the force and beauty of the style.

Wiclif's writings mark an epoch in the development of the English language. Chaucer did much for it; but his poems could not influence the people in the same way that Wiclif's Bible did. Nothing else could have the same intimate relation with the spiritual life of the people as the Bible, a new book to most of them. No words could so firmly fix themselves in their memory as those in which their Saviour had taught them the meaning and the duties of their life.

The first translation of the Bible was soon found to be very faulty. It was revised with great care by Wiclif himself, and more especially by his friend John Purveys. It was not complete in its new and greatly improved form till after Wiclif's death.

The Lollards, as the followers of Wiclif were called, formed a strong party, and their fervour did not begin to die out till the end of Henry V.'s reign; but we cannot doubt that the movement would have had more permanent results, had it not been interrupted by the Peasants' Revolt.

With the remainder of Richard II.'s reign we have nothing to do. We have only thought it right to trace briefly the movement amongst the working classes, which was the most important consequence of the Black Death.

In Wiclif's teaching and in the Peasants' Revolt we see the two most striking events of this epoch. In a certain way they were the results of the French wars, whose course we have been following. These wars produced a general stir and ferment; they gave the people new ideas and new life. The men who had earned such distinction by their brave fighting at Cressy and Poitiers were not content to settle down on their return home to the old state of things. They wanted greater freedom, better wages, an improved manner of living; their minds were open to receive new teaching. The result was the increasing discontent with their position, which led to the Peasants' Revolt, and the eagerness with which Wiclif's teaching was received on all sides.

But both Wiclif's teaching and the views expressed by the leaders of the Peasants' Revolt were premature. They were founded upon principles which could not at that time meet with general acceptance, and they were followed by a decided reaction. A period of darkness followed this great burst of intellectual life. In literature there were no worthy successors of Chaucer. The reforming views of Wiclif were slowly stamped out. The peasants failed in obtaining those results for which they had struggled. From the time of Chaucer till the days of the Reformation there is no great name in the history of English literature. It was not till then that intellectual life revived in England, and England took those great steps in advance which Wiclif had hoped she might take in his day. But we must not look upon the Reformation as in any way the result of Wiclif's teaching. By that time his ideas had faded away from men's remembrance, and the English Reformation received its impulse from Luther's teaching in Germany.

Even in this way the influence of the French wars was transient. The advantages which Edward III. and the Black Prince gained by their victories were lost, even in their own lifetime. In the same manner, the intellectual movement produced by these wars was stamped out, and was followed only by the long anarchy of the wars of the Roses.

www.ingramcontent.com/pod-product-compliance
Lightning Source LLC
Chambersburg PA
CBHW021005090426
42738CB00007B/657